Travel through time with the wonders of the world

- Discover the seven wonders of both the ancient and modern world, as well as many others, through coloring illustrations !

- From the Great Pyramid of Giza in Egypt to the Colosseum in Rome, and even to the city of Machu Picchu in Peru, immerse yourself in the history of architectural wonders that have stood the test of time.

- From the impressive Great Wall of China to the Taj Mahal in India, and even to the Temple of Artemis in Turkey, discover the engineering masterpieces that have dazzled audiences throughout the centuries.

- Color your way through the history of the seven wonders of the ancient and modern world and uncover the innovations that were required to achieve these incredible feats.

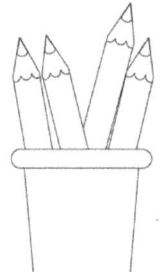

TO YOUR PENCILS !

Author : Jimmy VIGNALI

THE SEVEN WONDERS OF THE ANCIENT WORLD

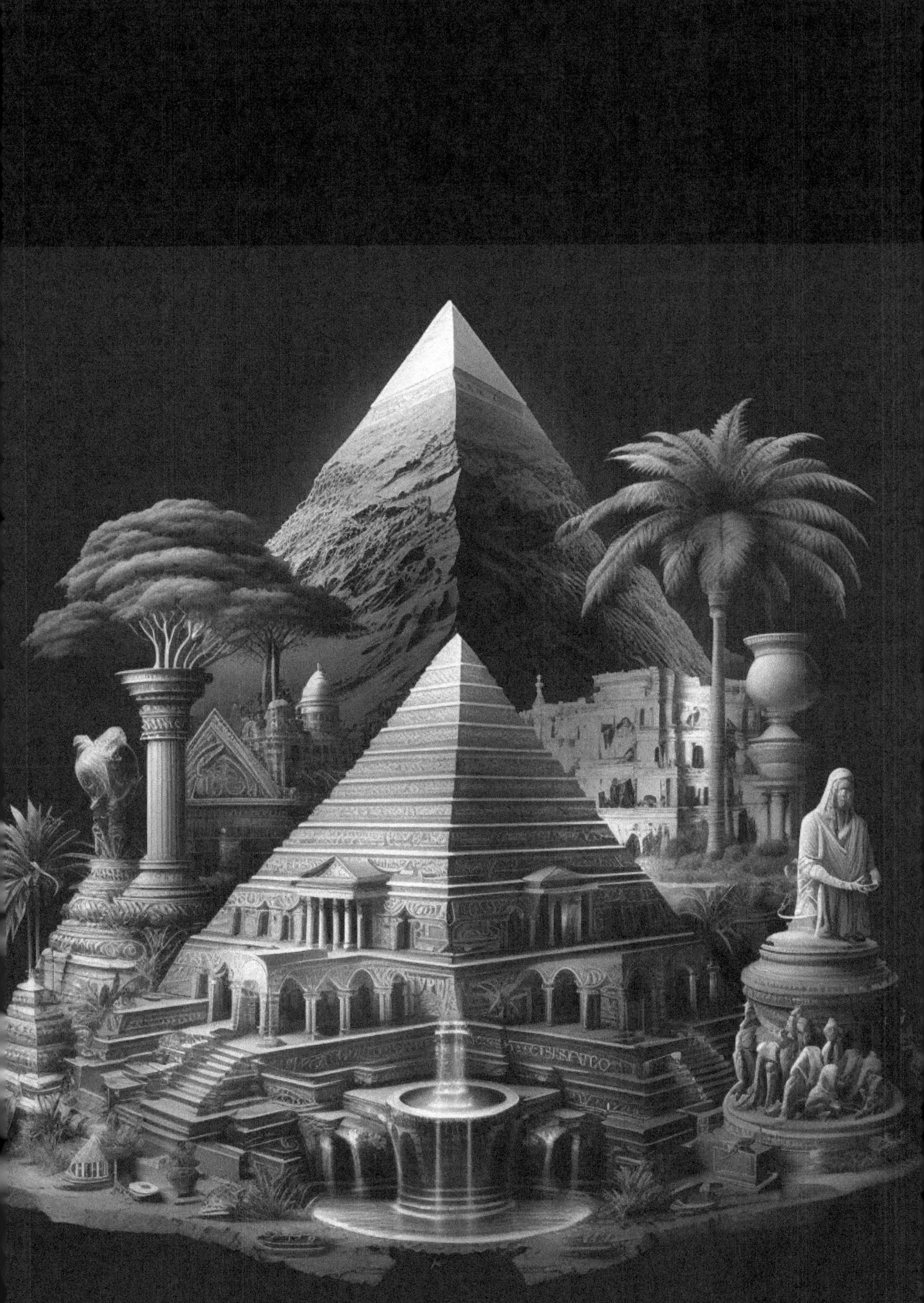

The Pyramid of Khufu

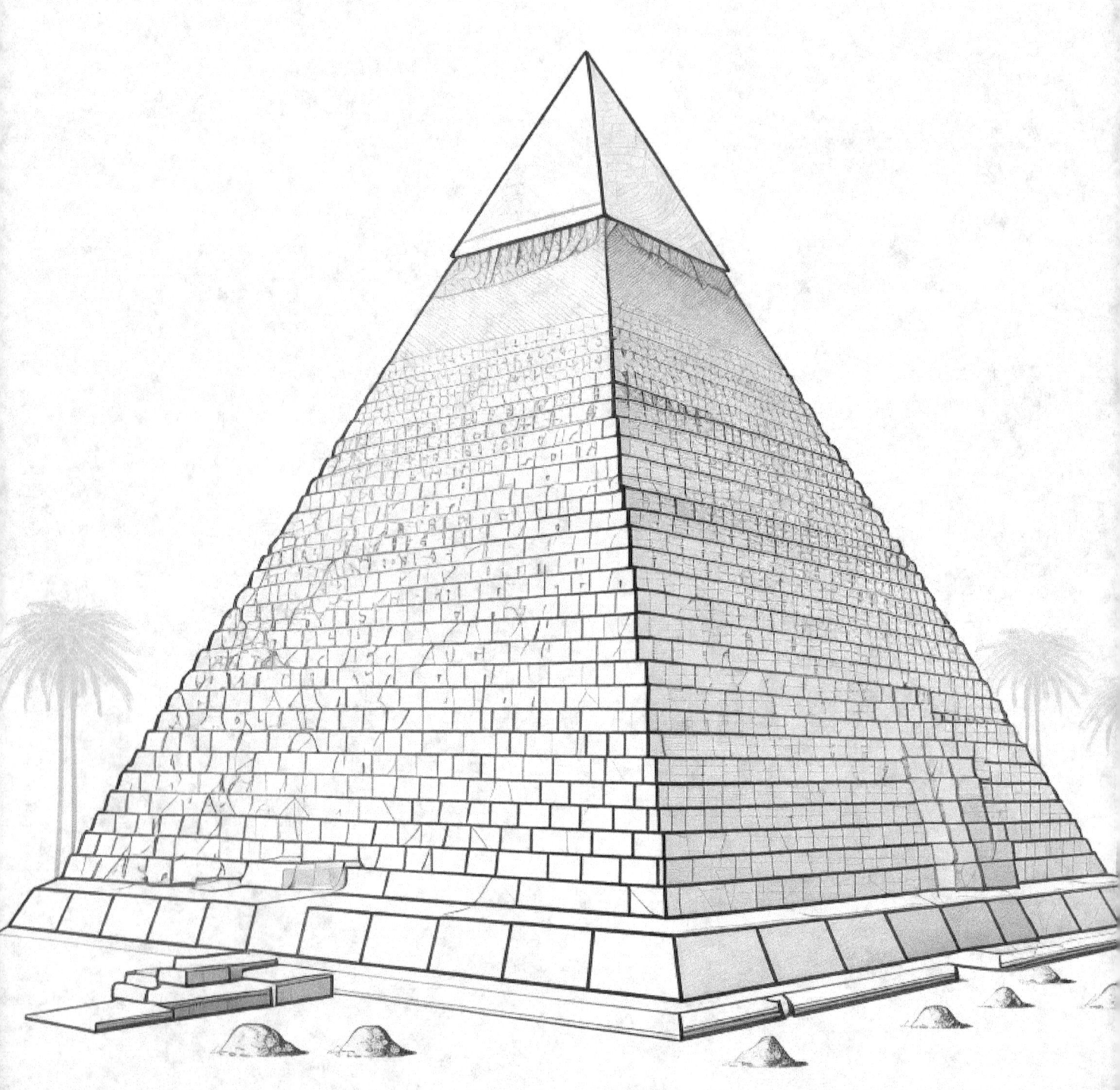

A historical treasure that continues to amaze the world

The Pyramid of Khufu is an iconic monument of ancient Egypt. Built over 4,500 years ago, this pyramid is the largest of all the pyramids of Giza, reaching a height of 146 meters. It is also one of the most impressive examples of the engineering and technology of the ancient Egyptians.

The construction method of the Pyramid of Khufu remains a mystery. However, it is accepted that the Egyptians used stone tools to quarry the limestone blocks and transport them to the pyramid site. Additionally, theories suggest that the Egyptians used ramps to drag the stone blocks to the top of the pyramid or used a sophisticated system of levers and pulleys to lift these massive blocks.

In addition to its mysterious construction, the Pyramid of Khufu is surrounded by many fascinating legends and anecdotes. For example, some have suggested that the pyramid contained secret chambers or hidden passages, although this has not been proven. Additionally, a popular legend tells that the pyramid was built by slaves. However, it is now widely accepted that the workers who built the pyramid were well-paid and respected laborers.

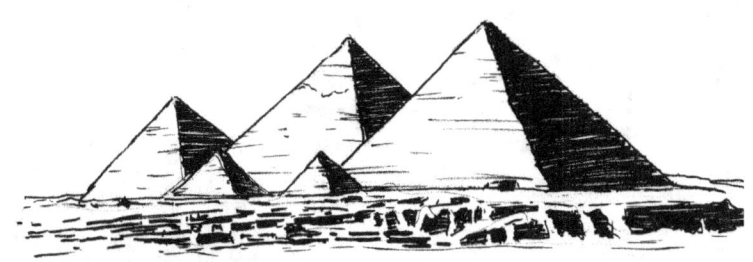

The Hanging Gardens of Babylon

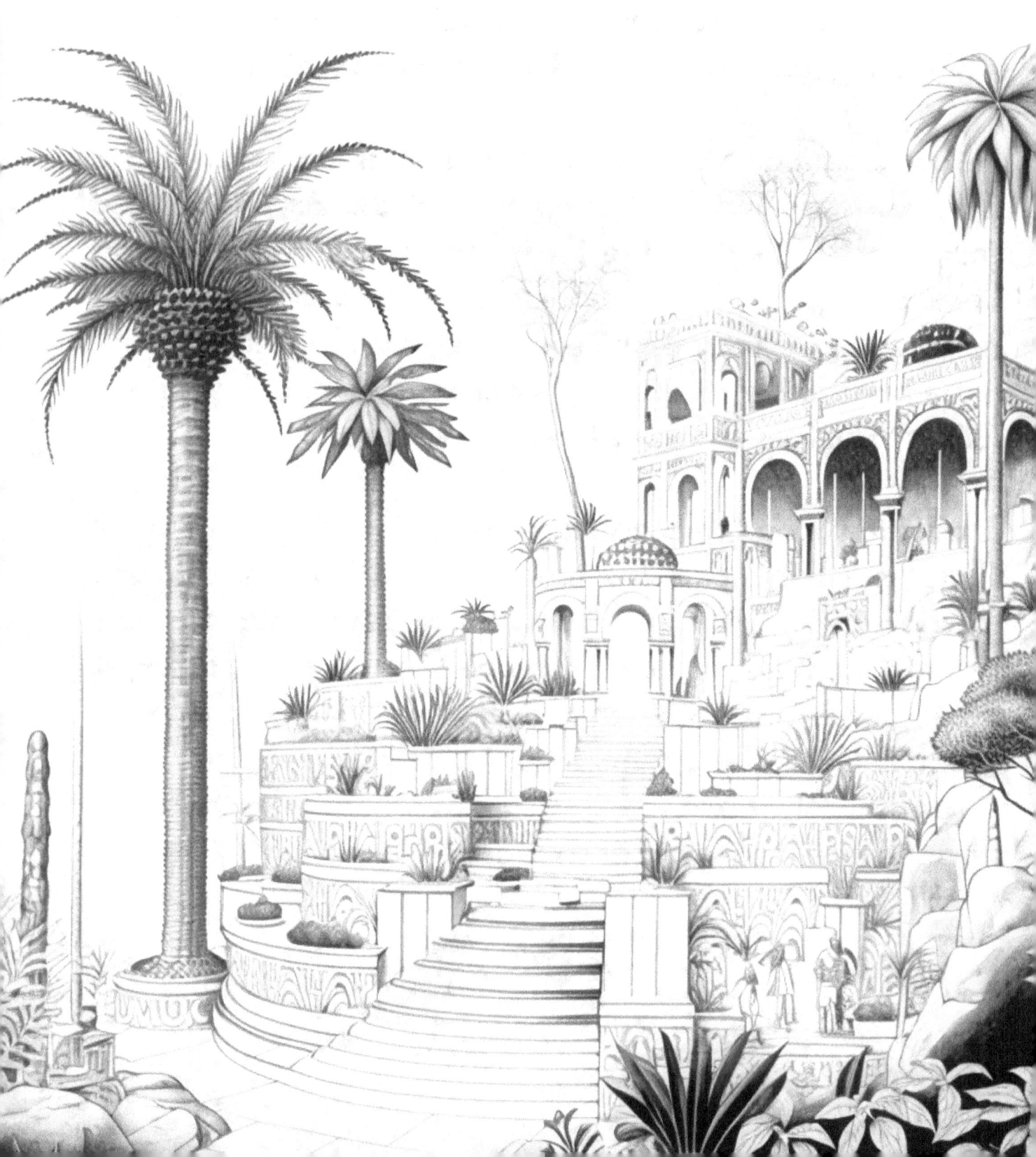

When vegetation reaches new heights

The Hanging Gardens of Babylon were one of the wonders of the ancient world, a remarkable structure of Babylonian civilization. According to legend, King Nebuchadnezzar II ordered their construction for his queen, who was nostalgic for the mountains of her homeland.

The construction method of the Hanging Gardens remains a topic of debate among historians. Some have suggested that the gardens were built on terraces, while others have proposed that they were actually floating gardens, suspended in the air with the help of sophisticated lifting systems. Whatever the method used, the gardens were renowned for their beauty and complexity, housing a wide variety of plants and trees.

It is said that the gardens were built to impress the queen, who was of Persian origin and accustomed to lush gardens. Additionally, some have suggested that the Hanging Gardens were equipped with a sophisticated irrigation system, powered by a series of canals and water pumps.

Unfortunately, the Hanging Gardens of Babylon were destroyed over time, probably by foreign invasions and earthquakes. Today, there is little trace of this wonder of antiquity, but their history and beauty continue to inspire and fascinate people around the world.

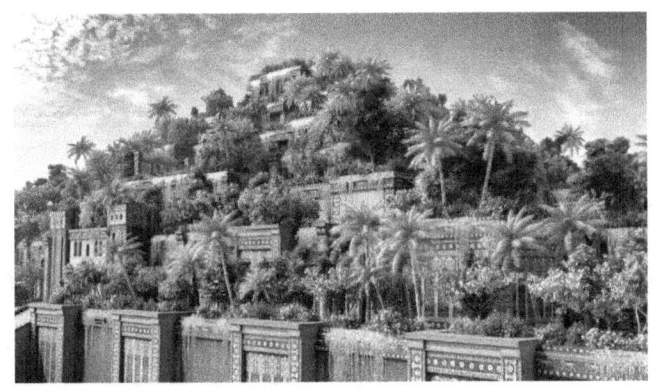

The Statue of Zeus

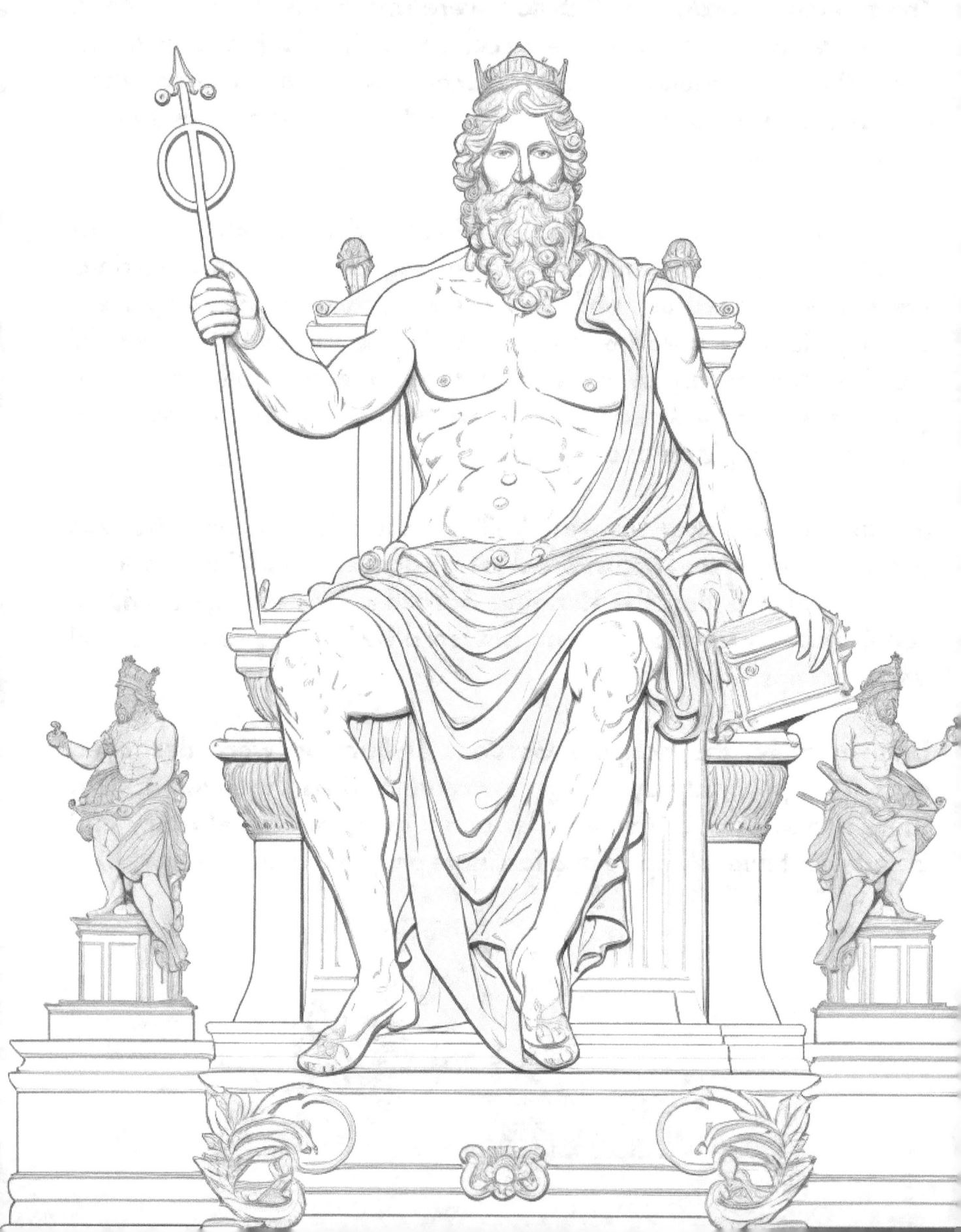

The statue that made mortals tremble

The statue of Zeus in gold and ivory, located in the Temple of Zeus in Olympia, was one of the seven wonders of the ancient world. The statue depicted the supreme god of Greek mythology, Zeus, seated on a throne and holding a scepter and a statue of Nike, the goddess of victory.

The method of construction of the statue remains a subject of debate, but it is believed to have been made using a wooden frame covered with ivory and gold. Skilled craftsmen worked for years to create this magnificent statue, which stood nearly 12 meters tall.

Fascinating anecdotes are associated with the statue of Zeus. It is said that the statue was so large and impressive that visitors were often overwhelmed by its divine aura. The famous Greek geographer Strabo described the statue as "a prodigy in gold, ivory, and stone, the work of Phidias, which so impressed and enchanted the spectators that they were all struck with wonder."
Unfortunately, the statue of Zeus was destroyed in the fire that consumed the temple in 426 CE, putting an end to one of the most remarkable wonders of antiquity.

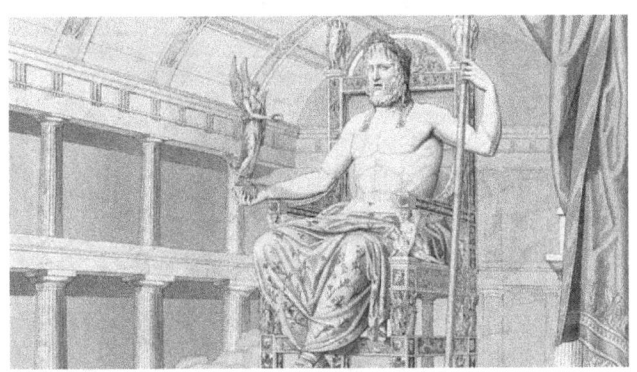

The Temple of Artemis

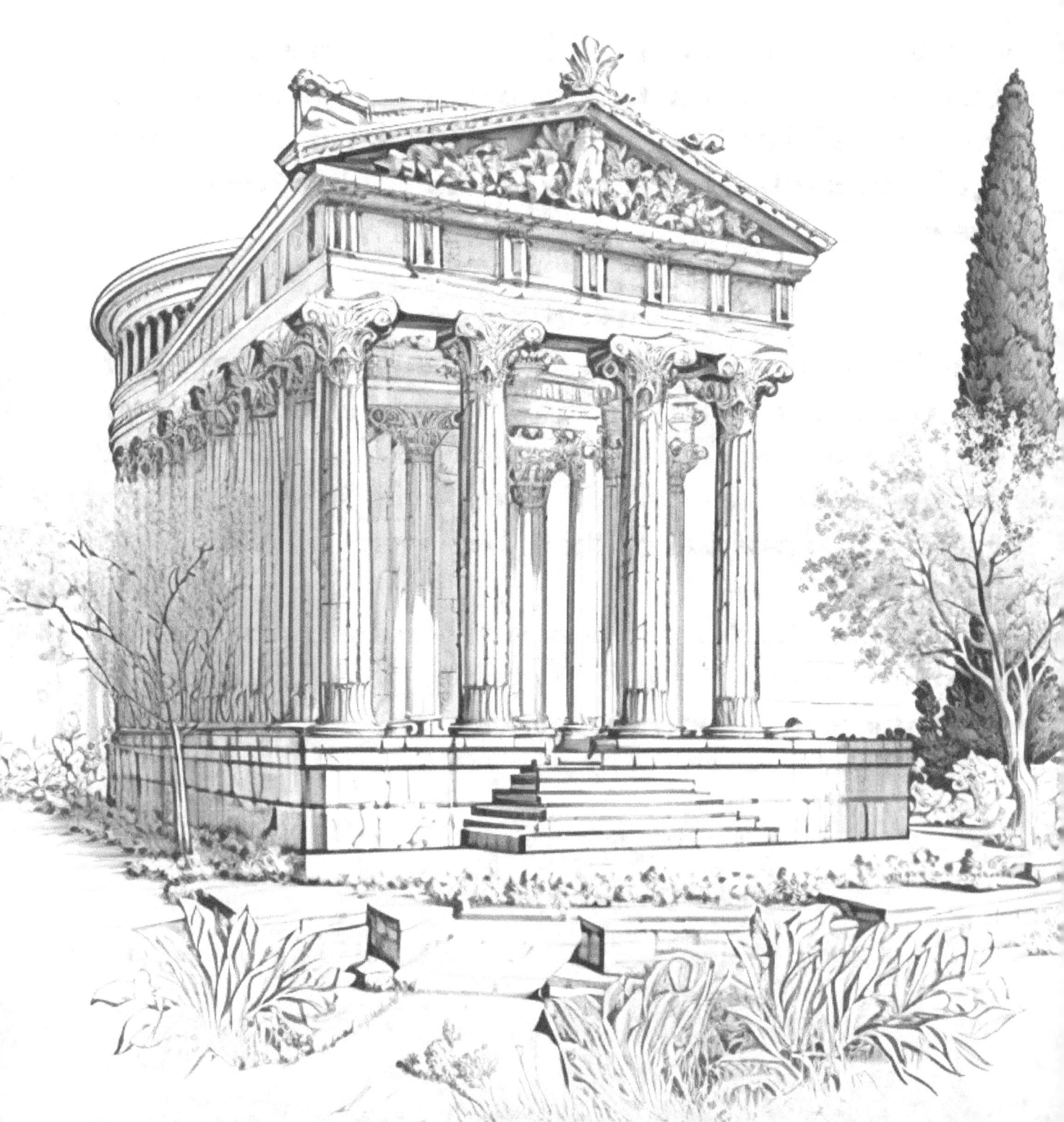

Artemis, the goddess of hunting, finds a home

The Temple of Artemis was built in the 6th century BCE in honor of the Greek goddess of hunting and nature, Artemis. It was a massive temple with over 100 marble columns that rose over 18 meters high.

The construction method was incredibly advanced for the time. The columns were carved from marble and assembled on-site using iron attachments. The walls were adorned with ivory and gold ornaments, making it one of the most lavish temples of antiquity.

There were several versions of the temple over the centuries, each one larger and more elaborate than the previous. However, despite its grandeur and beauty, the Temple of Artemis met a tragic end. In 356 BCE, it was destroyed in an arson attack by a man named Herostratus, who wanted to become famous. Alexander the Great later ordered its reconstruction, but the temple never regained its former glory.

Today, even though only ruins remain, the Temple of Artemis continues to inspire imagination and admiration.

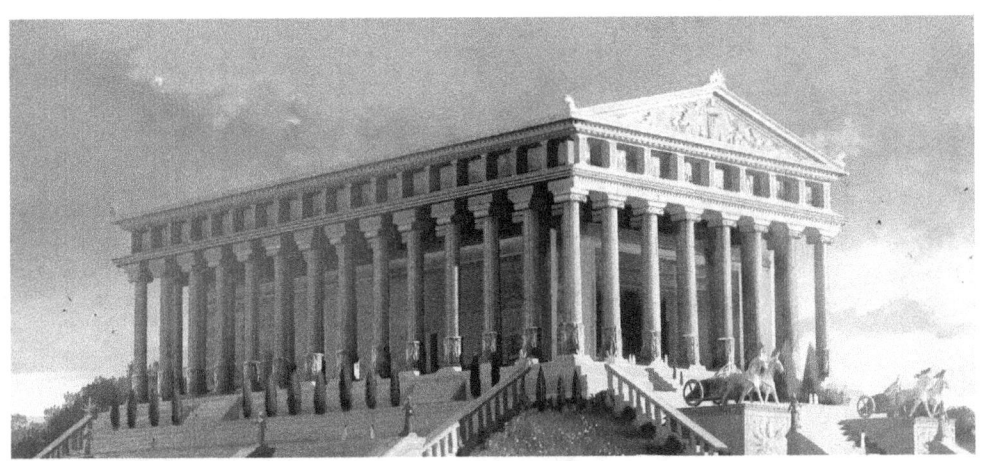

The Mausoleum at Halicarnassus

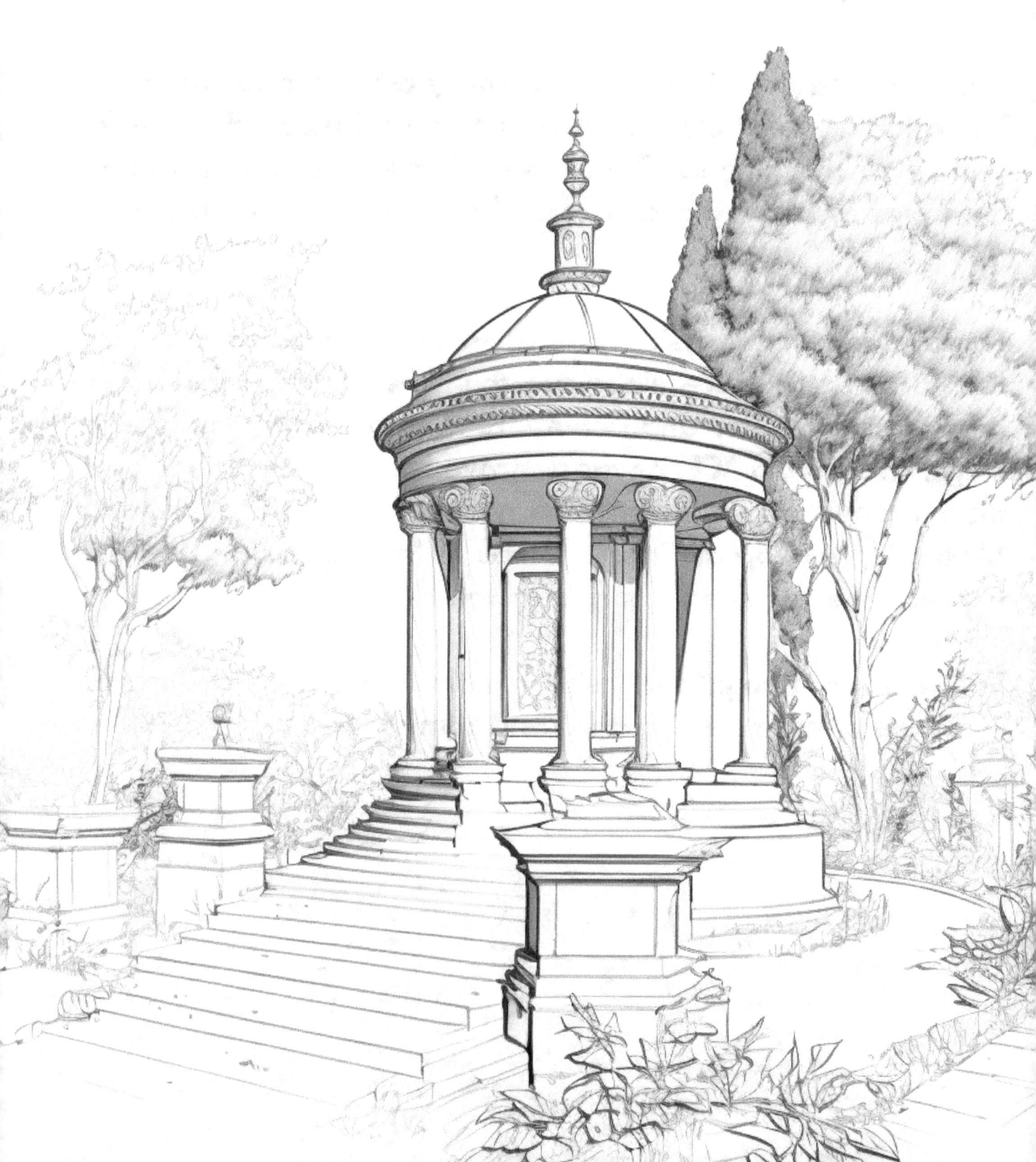

A death that impresses

The Mausoleum at Halicarnassus, built in the 4th century BCE in Turkey, was a more than 45-meter-high funerary monument adorned with magnificent sculptures depicting mythological scenes and battles.

The construction method was impressive, with stones weighing several tons assembled using levers and wheeled carts. The Greek sculptor Scopas created a statue of Artemisia, Mausolus's wife, so lifelike that visitors mistook it for a real person. The mausoleum suffered numerous damages over the centuries, and the Knights of St. John used the ruins to build their castle in the 15th century.

Although only ruins remain today, the Mausoleum at Halicarnassus had a significant influence on architecture and sculpture and allowed historians to better understand the life and culture of antiquity.

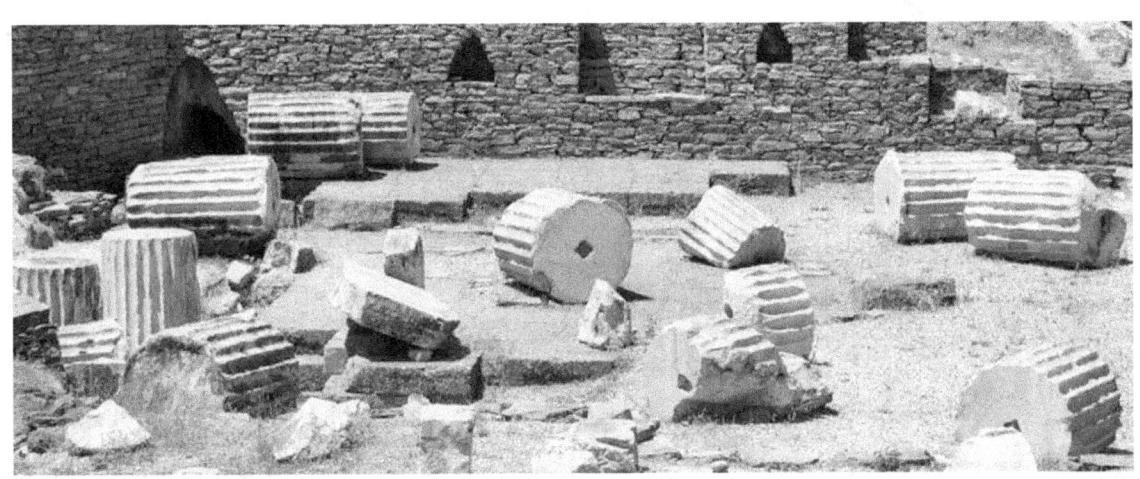

The Colossus of Rhodes

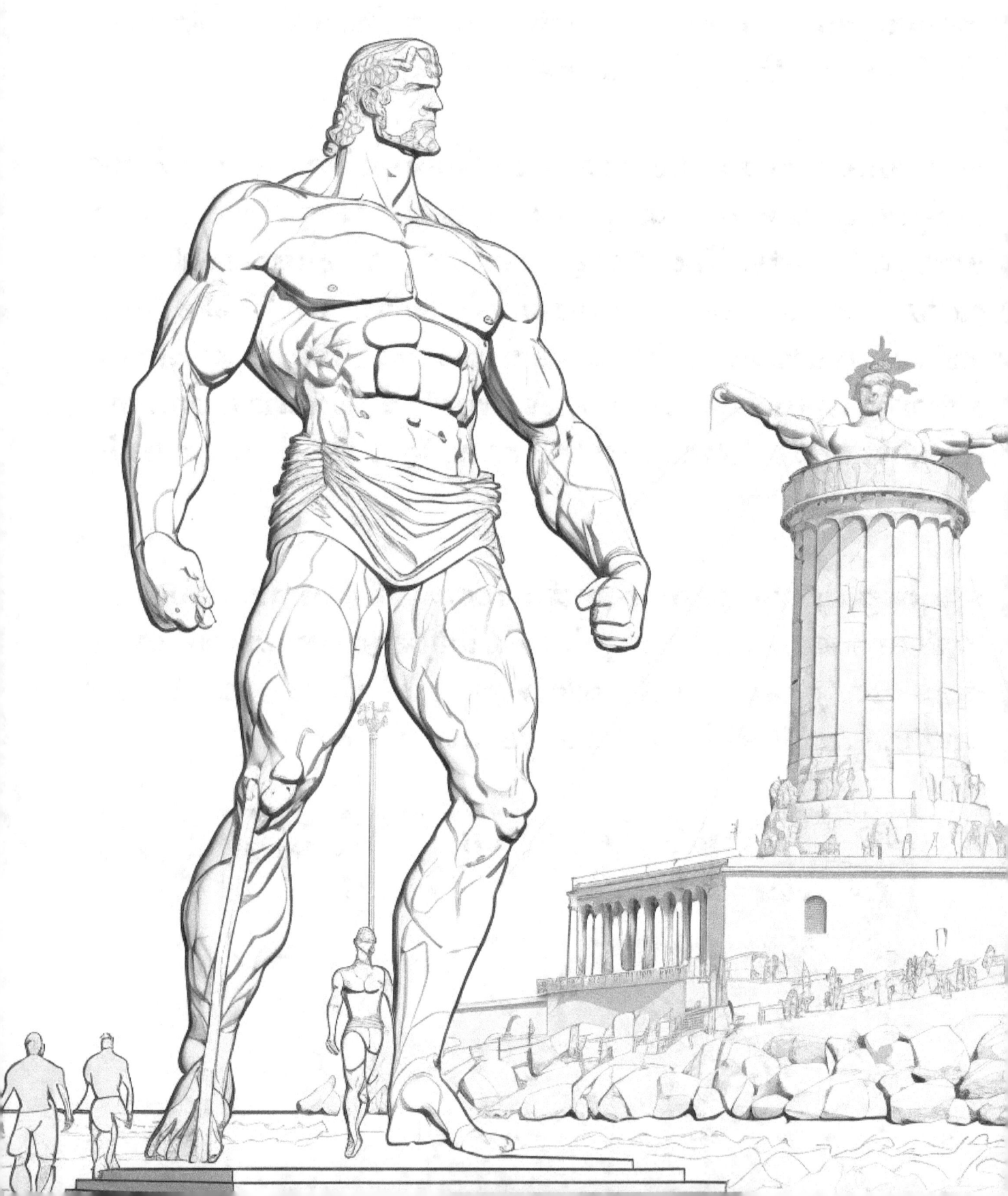

The Giant of Antiquity

The Giant of Antiquity: The Colossus of Rhodes was an ancient monumental bronze statue representing Helios, the Greek god of the sun. It was built between 292 and 280 BC to celebrate the victory of the Rhodians over the Macedonian army of Demetrius Poliorcetes.

The construction of the statue was supervised by the Greek sculptor Chares of Lindos. It stood approximately 33 meters high and was installed at the entrance of the port of Rhodes, one of the main sea routes of the time. The Rhodians used innovative construction techniques to erect the statue, including the use of a wooden framework to support the structure during its construction.

An earthquake in 226 BC damaged the statue, causing it to fall into pieces. The remains were left in place for nearly 900 years before the Arabs recovered them and melted them down to make coins.

Although it no longer exists today, reproductions of the statue have been created over the centuries in an attempt to recreate its grandeur and majesty. Thus, the Colossus of Rhodes has remained in the collective imagination, inspiring tales of travelers and artistic representations throughout history.

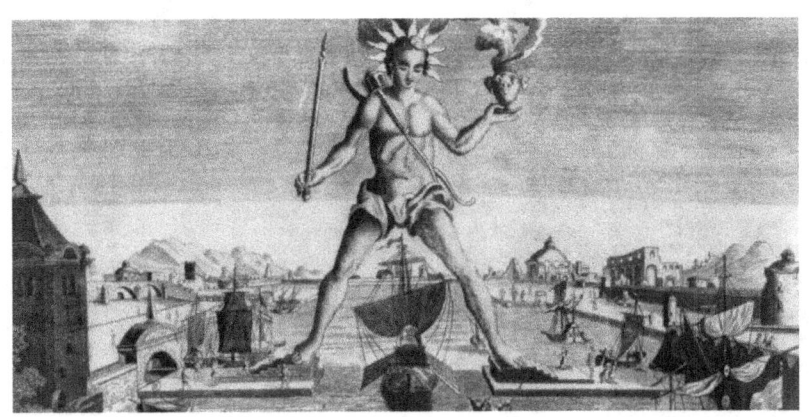

The Lighthouse of Alexandria

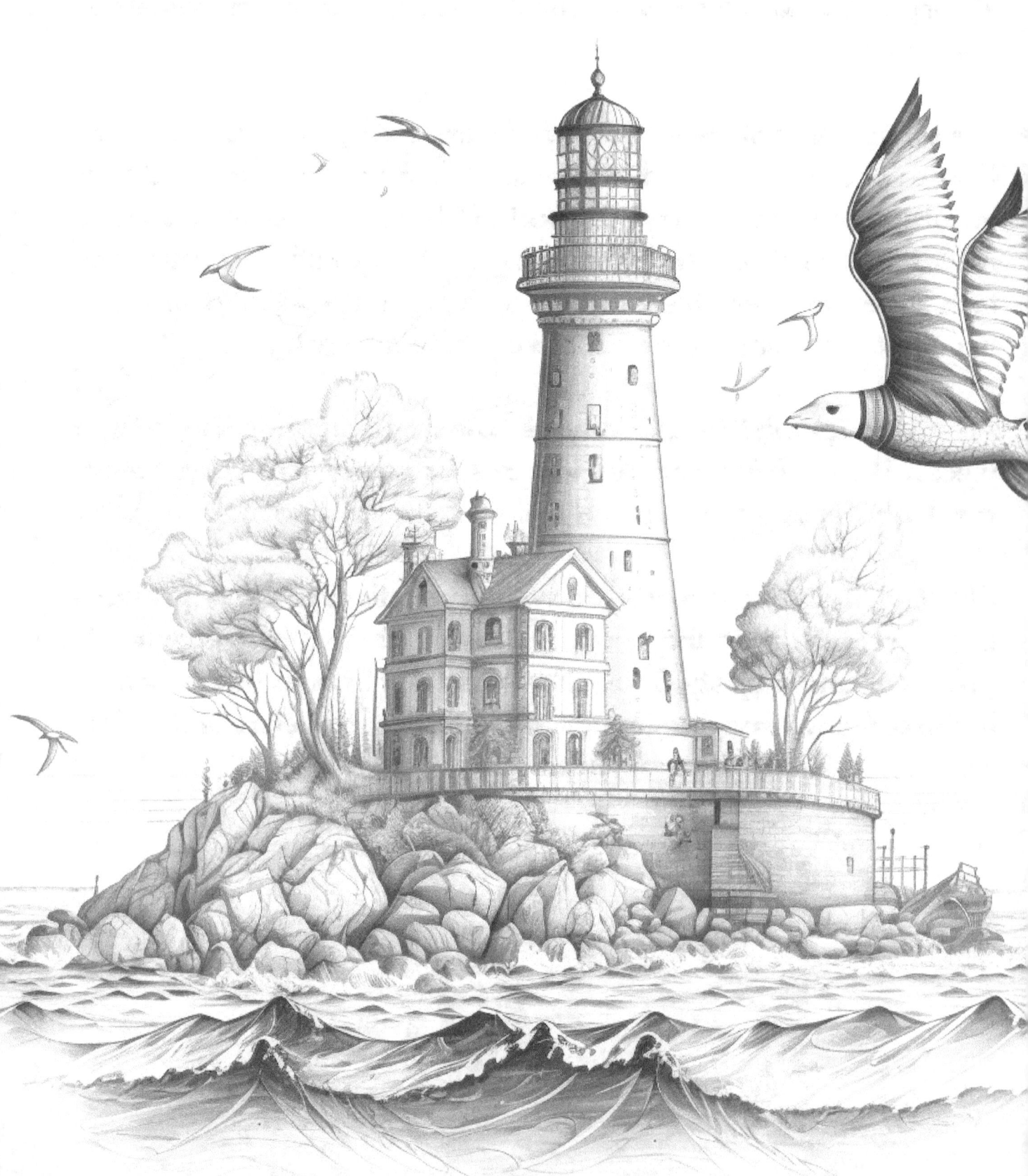

The wonder that illuminated the world

The Lighthouse of Alexandria was an immense 130-meter-tall lighthouse built in Alexandria, Egypt, in the 3rd century BCE. Its construction was ordered by Ptolemy I, founder of the Ptolemaic dynasty, to guide ships entering and leaving the port of Alexandria.

The construction of the lighthouse was made with blocks of limestone, granite, and marble. The tower was designed to be visible from over 50 kilometers at sea, with an immense bronze lantern at its top that burned fires to guide ships.

The Lighthouse of Alexandria is considered one of the greatest architectural achievements of antiquity. Unfortunately, the lighthouse was destroyed in an earthquake in 1303 AD. The stone blocks were recovered and used for other constructions, but its fame remained intact. The Lighthouse of Alexandria became a source of inspiration for architects, artists, and writers for centuries. Today, it is considered one of the Seven Wonders of the Ancient World.

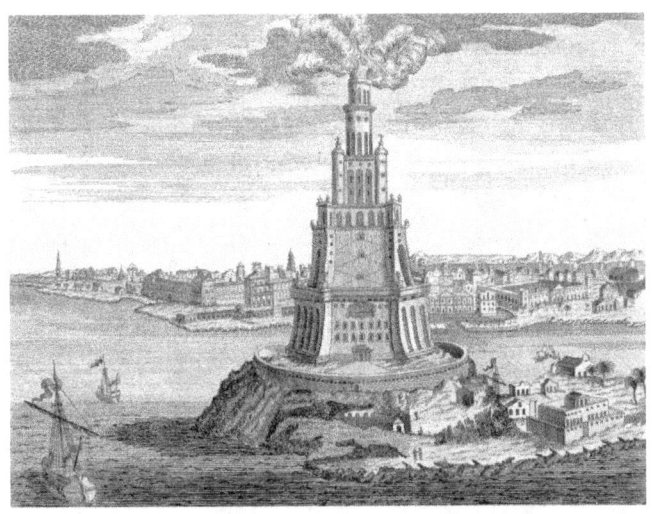

THE 7 MODERN WONDERS OF THE WORLD

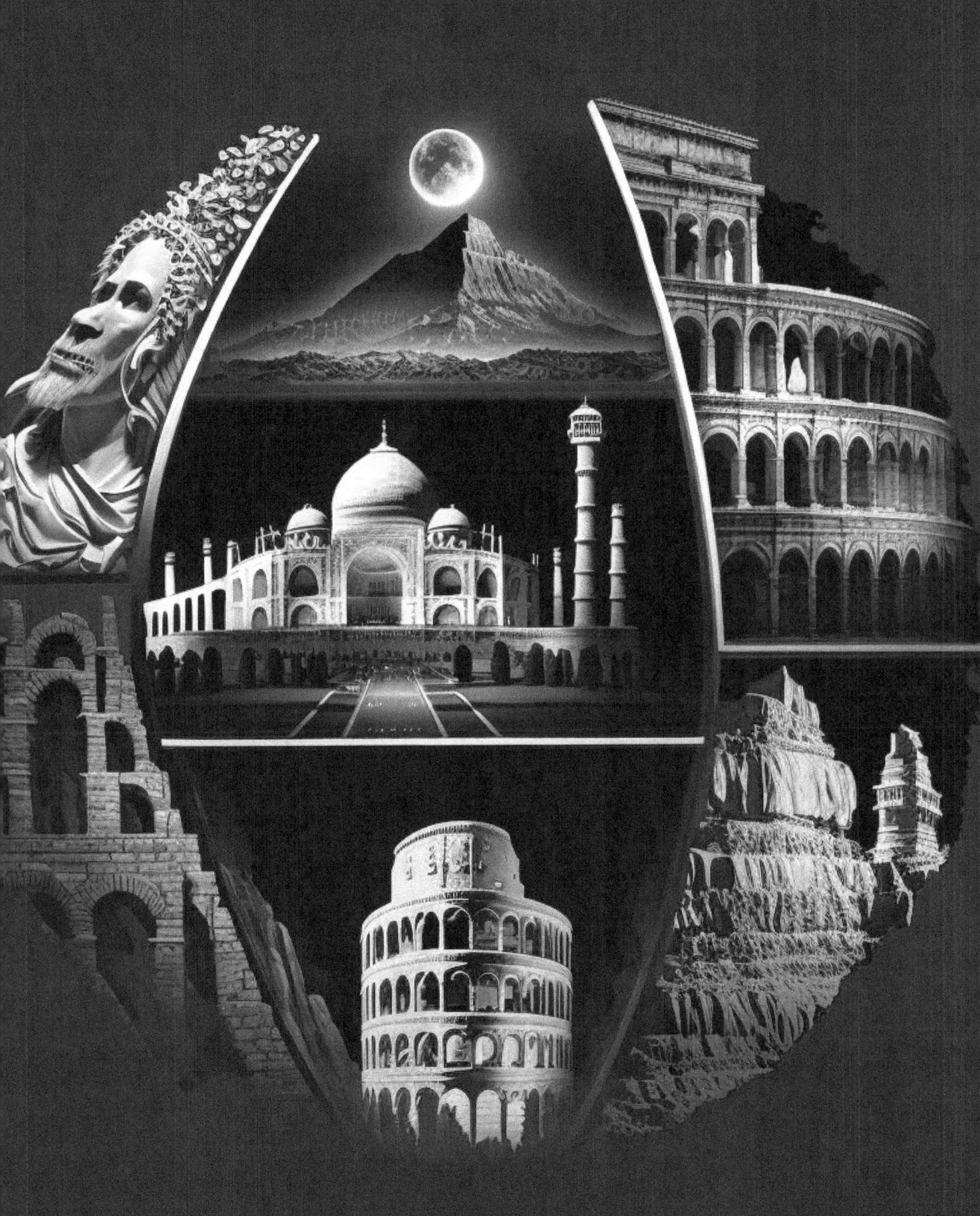

The Taj Mahal

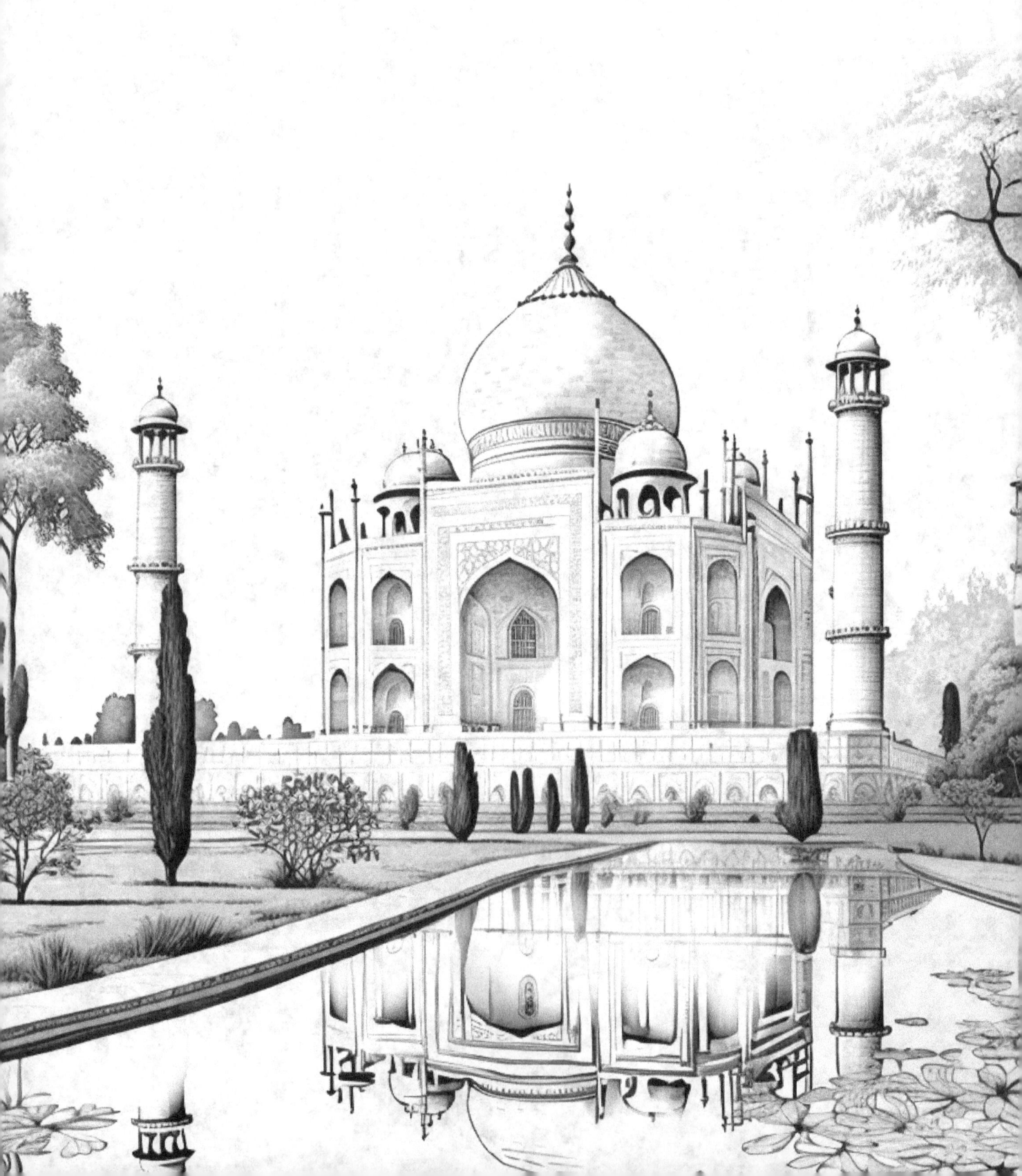

Love can build wonders

The Taj Mahal is a mausoleum located in Agra, India, built in the 17th century by the Mughal Emperor Shah Jahan in memory of his beloved wife, Mumtaz Mahal, who died while giving birth to their fourteenth child.

Construction of the Taj Mahal began in 1632 and lasted 22 years. The complex includes a garden, a mosque, and a grand entrance gate, but the main building is the tomb of Mumtaz Mahal. The mausoleum is constructed of finely carved white marble, inlaid with precious stones and floral motifs.

Emperor Shah Jahan had planned to build a Taj Mahal in black marble on the other side of the Yamuna River, facing the white Taj Mahal. This project was never realized due to a succession war among Shah Jahan's sons.

The Taj Mahal has become one of the most famous and visited monuments in India, attracting millions of visitors each year. It is considered one of the most extraordinary examples of Mughal architecture and was designated a UNESCO World Heritage Site in 1983.

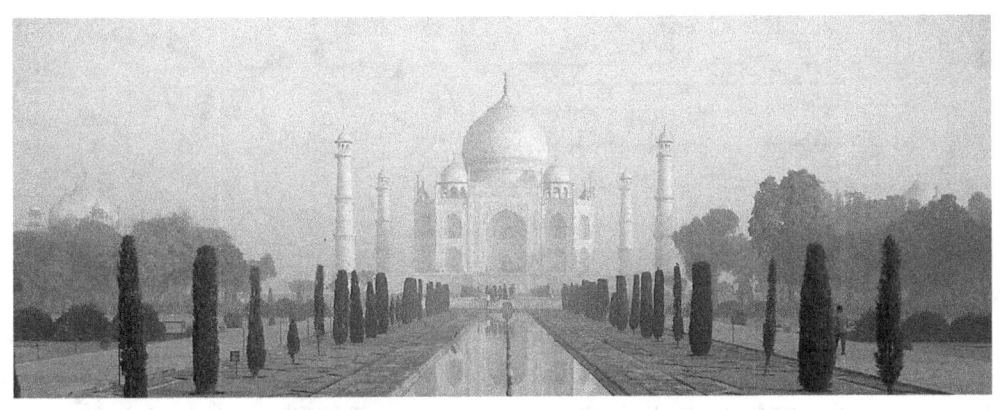

The Great Wall of China

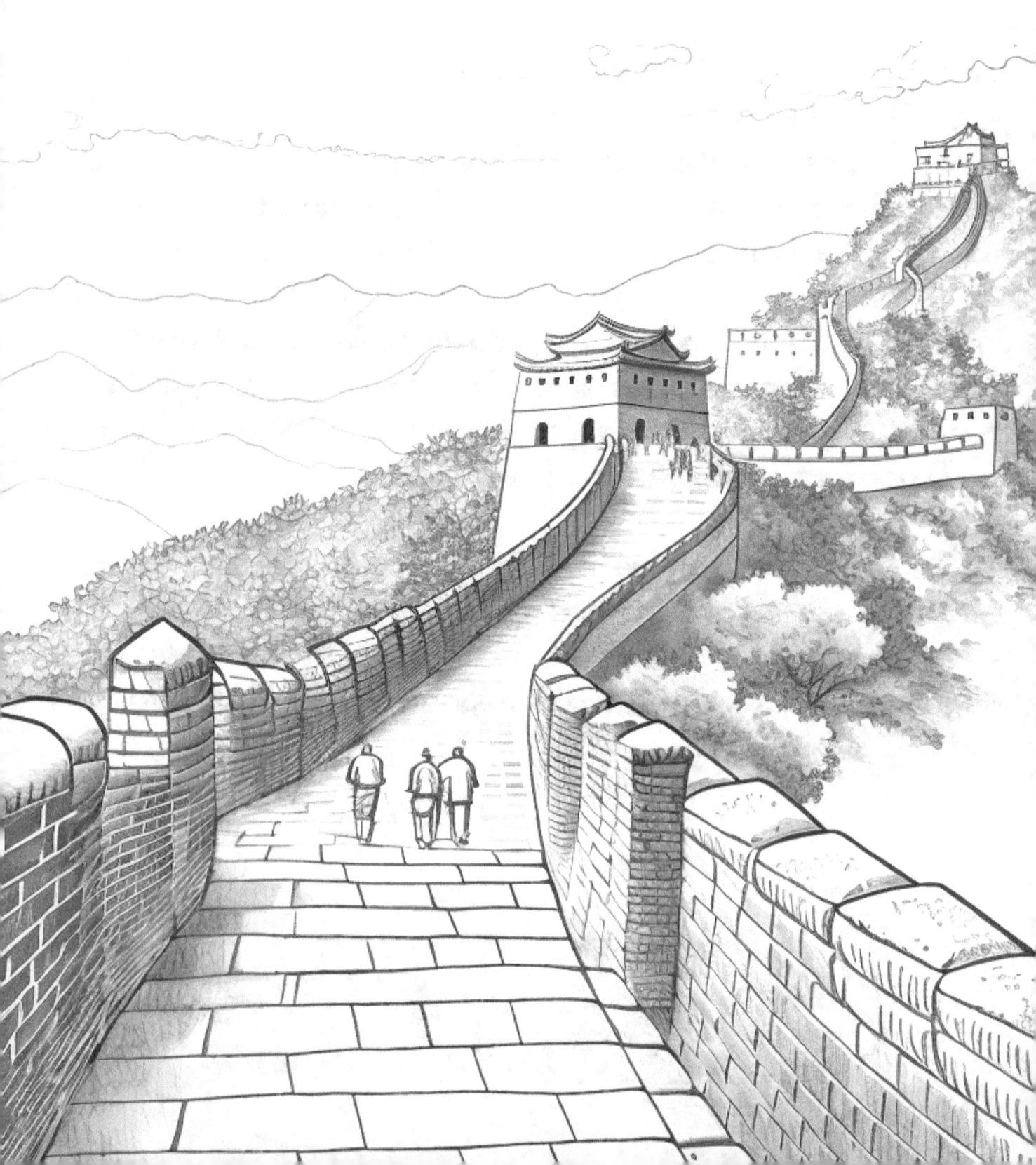

The longest wall in the world

The Great Wall of China is a series of fortifications built over centuries by Chinese emperors to protect their territory against invaders from the north. The construction of the Great Wall began in the 7th century BCE and continued for over 2,000 years, with additions and renovations made by different dynasties.

The construction method of the Great Wall was primarily based on the use of bricks, stones, wood, and earth. Workers used simple tools such as wheelbarrows, shovels, and picks to transport and build the materials. A technique known as "jian" (interlocking) was also used to assemble stones like a puzzle.

The Great Wall of China has become one of the most famous wonders of the world and one of the most popular tourist attractions in China. It stretches over 21,000 km through the mountains and valleys of northern China and is considered one of the greatest achievements in the history of engineering and architecture. The Great Wall was designated a UNESCO World Heritage Site in 1987.

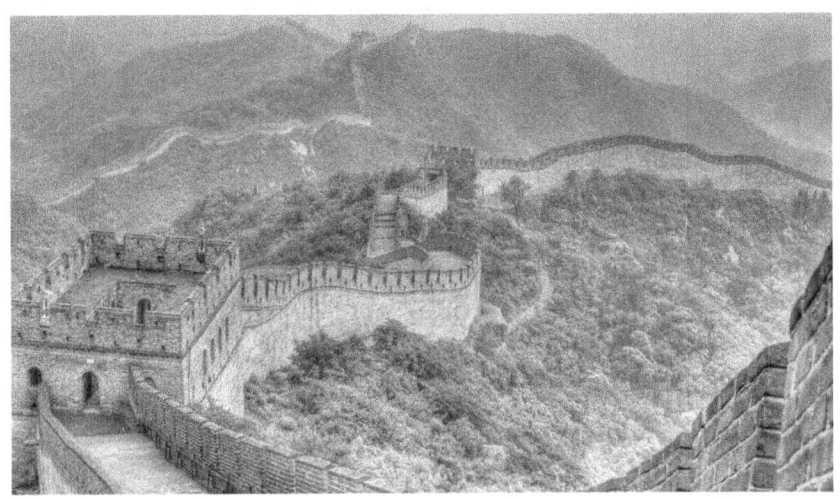

City of Petra

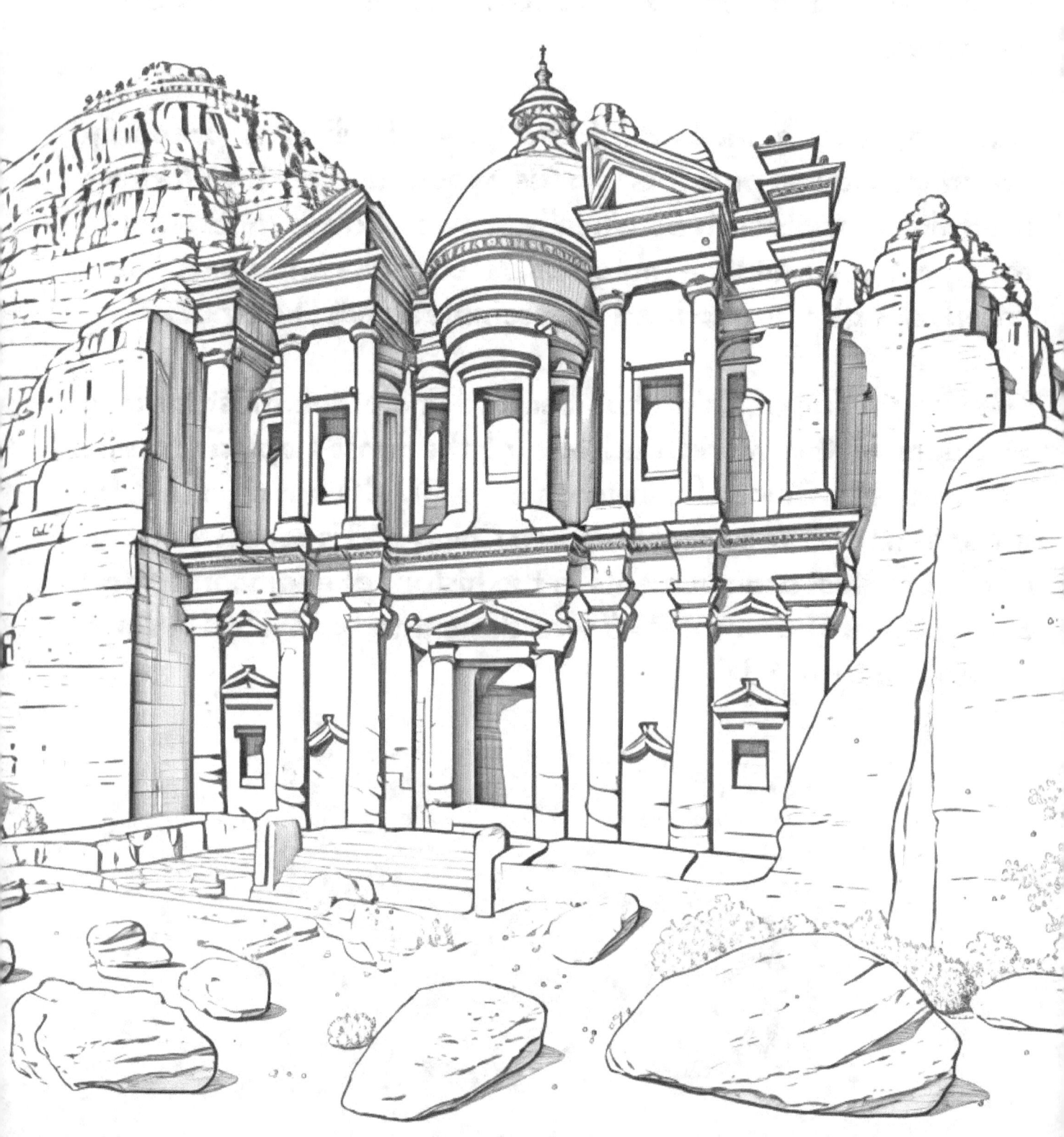

Carved in the rock

Petra, located in Jordan, is a marvel of ancient architecture. The city was founded in the 6th century BCE by the Nabataeans, a nomadic Arab people. It is famous for its temples, tombs, and houses carved into the rock.

The construction method of Petra was based on the use of the local rock called pink sandstone. The Nabataeans carved monumental structures into the sandstone cliffs to create their city. They also developed a sophisticated system of canals to transport potable water from distant sources.

The Nabataeans used their ingenuity to build tunnels and canals to evacuate rainwater to prevent flooding and ensure a constant water supply. They also built cistern systems to store potable water during periods of drought.

Petra is a UNESCO World Heritage Site since 1985 and has become a popular tourist destination due to its beauty and fascinating history. It is also known for being the location of several Hollywood films, including Indiana Jones and the Last Crusade.

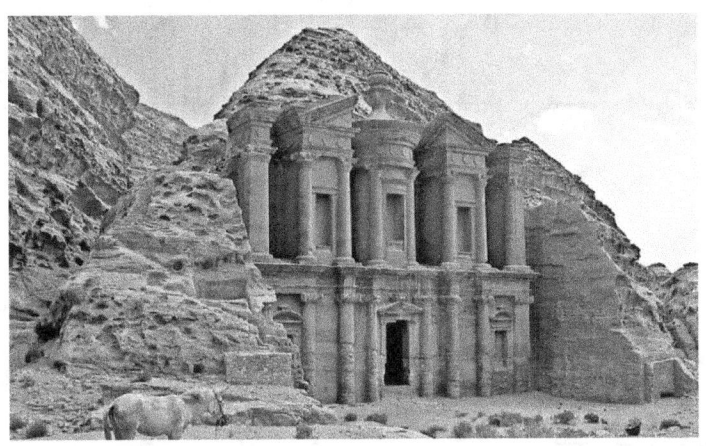

The Christ the Redeemer statue

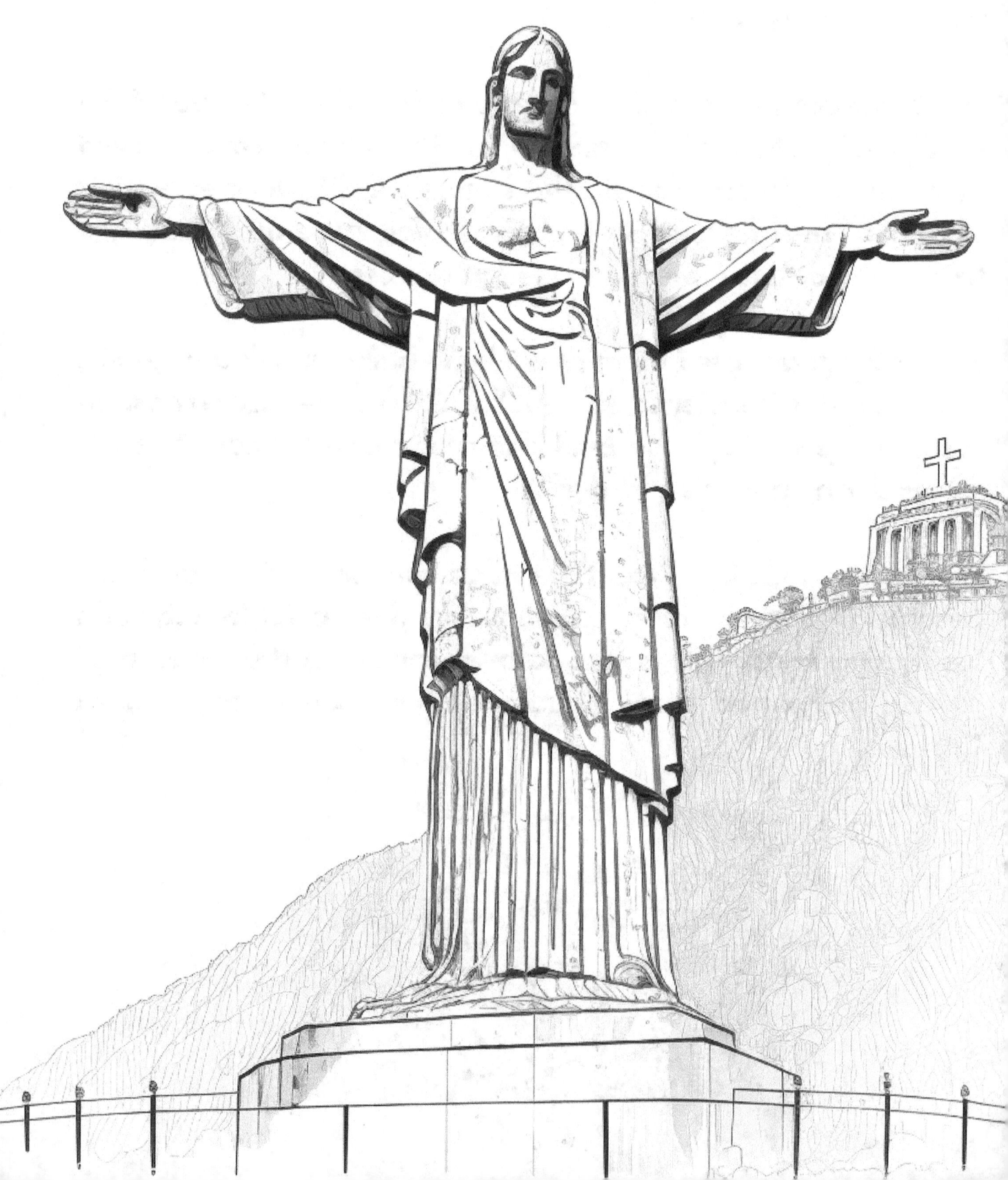

The statue that offers a divine view

The Christ the Redeemer statue is an iconic monument located in Rio de Janeiro, Brazil. This 30-meter tall statue is perched on top of the Corcovado mountain and attracts thousands of tourists every year.

The construction of the statue began in 1922 and was completed in 1931. The statue was designed by Brazilian engineer Heitor da Silva Costa, in collaboration with French sculptor Paul Landowski.

The construction of the statue was funded by donations from the Brazilian population and Catholics from around the world. The first stone was laid in 1922 by the Brazilian president of the time, Epitacio Pessoa, during a solemn ceremony.

Today, the statue has become an important cultural symbol for Brazil and is one of the seven wonders of the modern world.

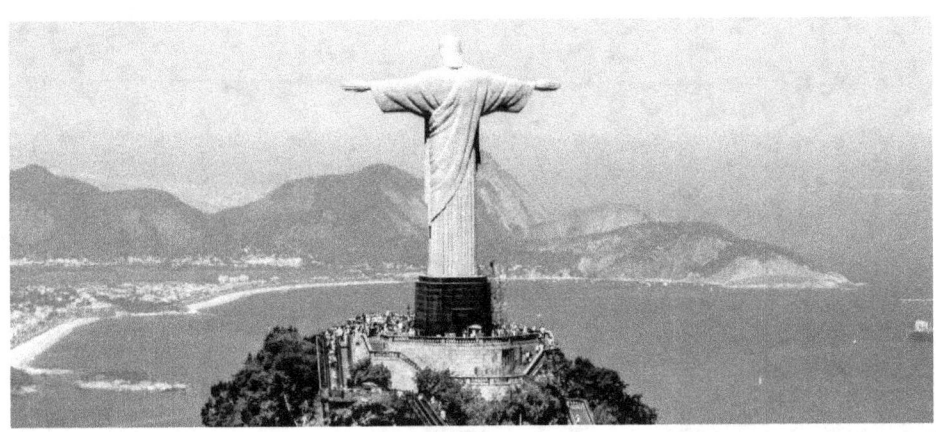

Machu Picchu

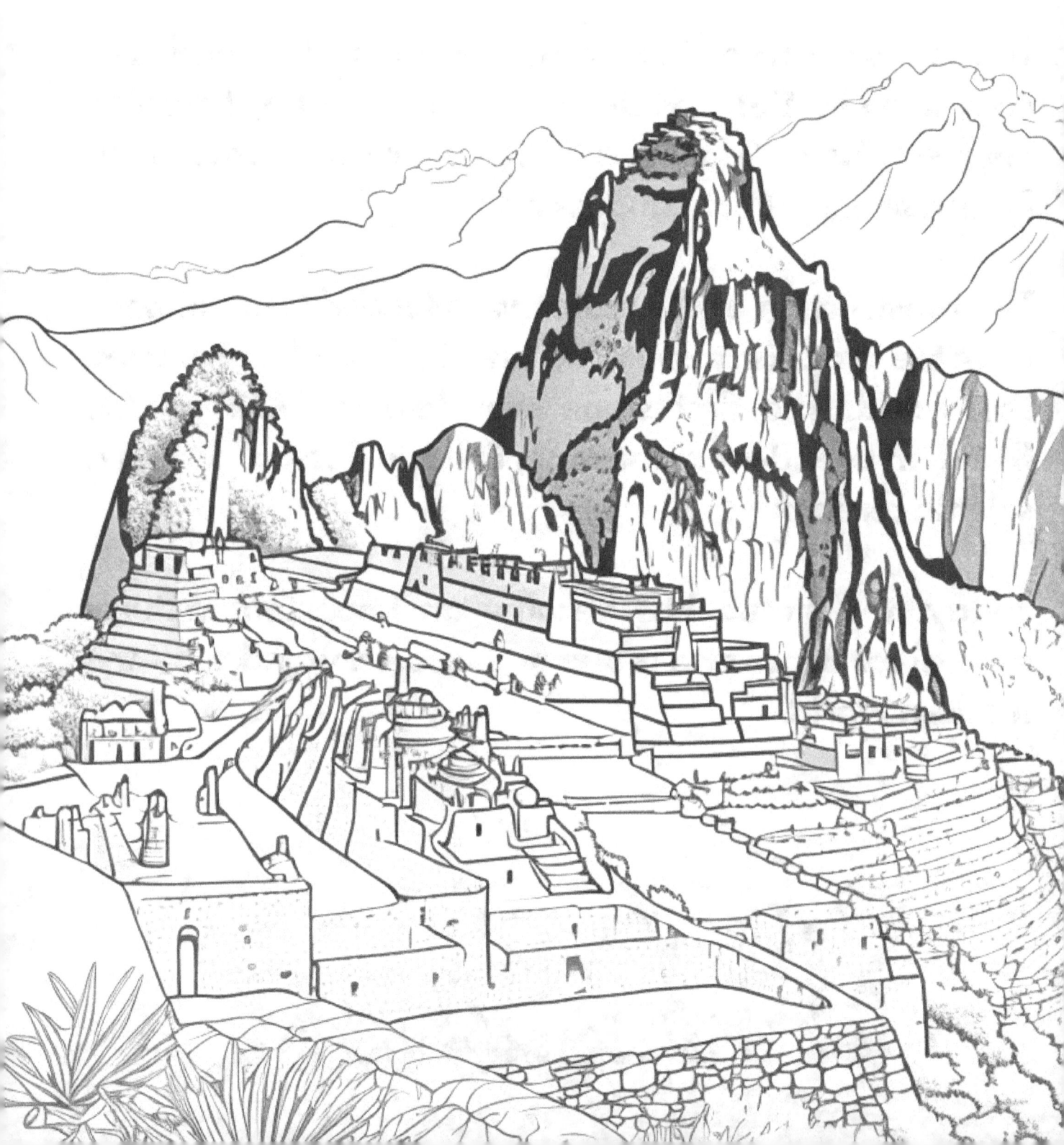

Where llamas reign supreme

Machu Picchu was built on a mountain ridge at an altitude of 2430 meters above sea level, and the construction was done without the use of mortar. The stones that make up the buildings were carefully cut to fit perfectly together.

The site includes many temples, palaces, and agricultural terraces, as well as a sophisticated canal system that transported water from the mountains to the city.

Machu Picchu was discovered in 1911 by American archaeologist Hiram Bingham. Although he initially thought the site was the legendary Vilcabamba, the last Inca city to resist Spanish conquistadors, he quickly realized it was an entirely different city.

Today, Machu Picchu is a popular tourist attraction, attracting thousands of visitors each year. It is also considered one of the seven wonders of the modern world and has been a UNESCO World Heritage site since 1983.

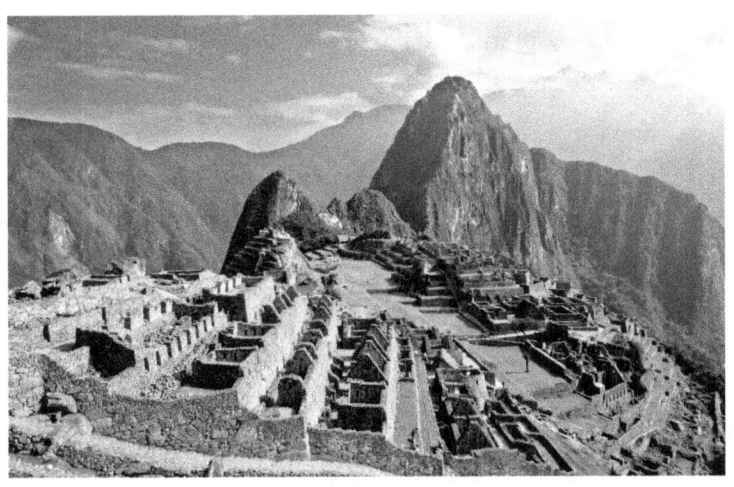

Archaeological site of Chichén Itzá

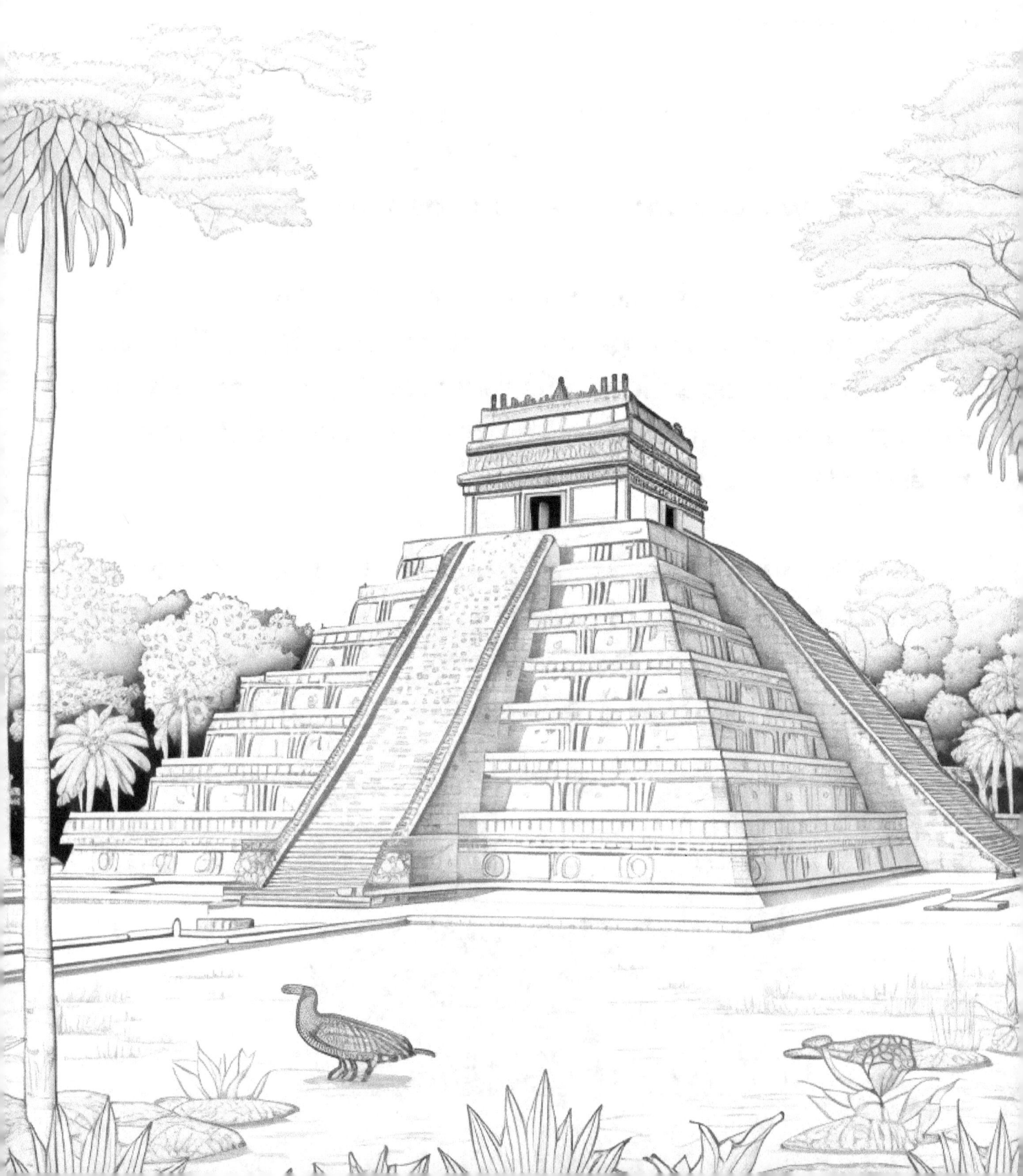

Largest amusement park of the Maya Empire

Chichén Itzá is an archaeological site located in the Yucatan Peninsula, Mexico, which was one of the major political and religious centers of the Mayan civilization. The city was founded in the 6th century and reached its peak between the 10th and 13th centuries. The site is famous for its complex architecture and sculptures, as well as for the astronomical alignments that were incorporated into the construction of the buildings.

The most famous structure in Chichén Itzá is probably the Kukulcán Pyramid, also known as "El Castillo". The pyramid is composed of nine terraces and measures about 30 meters high. It was built using an extremely precise leveling technique that allowed for perfect alignment of the four sides of the pyramid with the cardinal points.

Chichén Itzá is considered one of the most important archaeological sites in the Americas and has been designated as one of the seven wonders of the modern world.

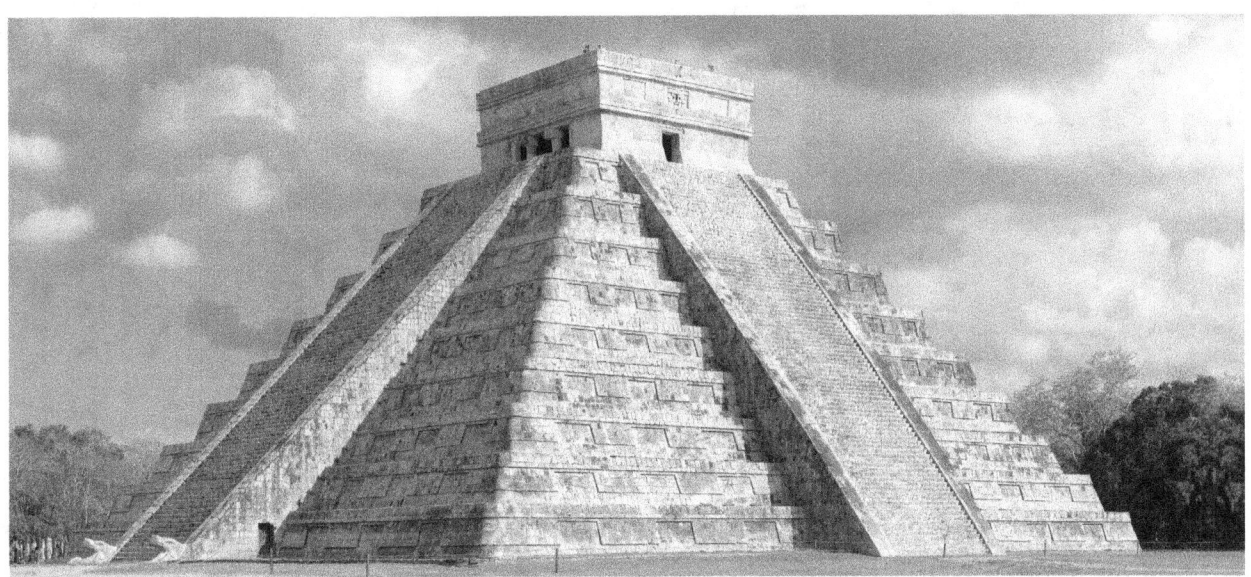

The Colosseum

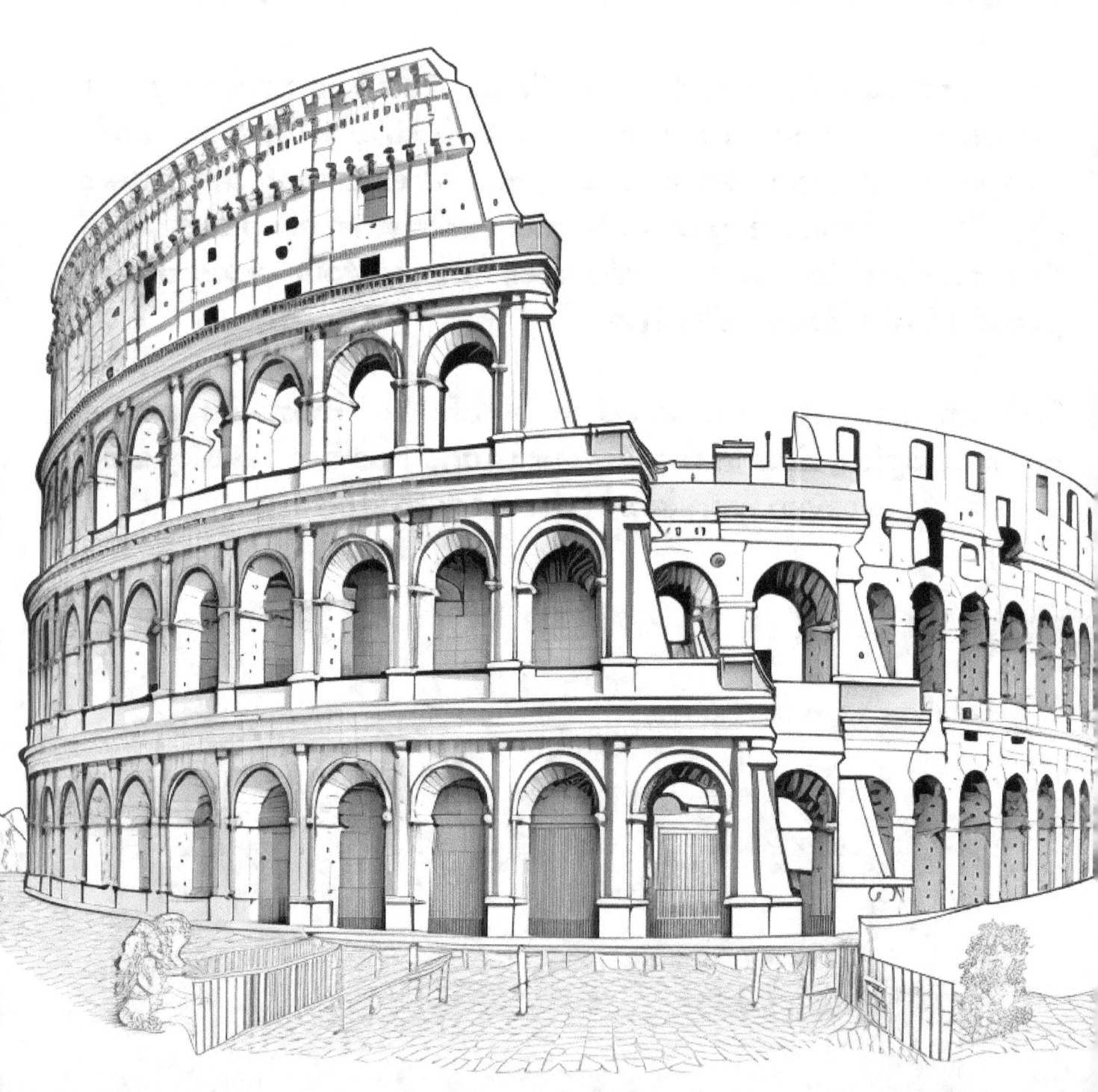

The playground of gladiators

The Colosseum is one of the most iconic monuments in Rome and a symbol of its glorious past. Built in the 1st century AD, the Colosseum was the largest amphitheater ever built and could accommodate up to 50,000 spectators. The construction method of the Colosseum was based on advanced techniques for the time, including the use of concrete, bricks, and cut stone.

The spectacles presented in the Colosseum were as varied as they were bloody, ranging from gladiator fights to reenactments of naval battles. The shows were organized by Roman emperors to entertain the population and strengthen their power. The Colosseum is also known for the Christian martyrs who were executed there during the first centuries of the Christian era.

Despite the centuries that have passed since its construction, the Colosseum still stands today, although partially in ruins. It continues to attract millions of visitors each year and remains a fascinating testament to the grandeur of the Roman Empire.

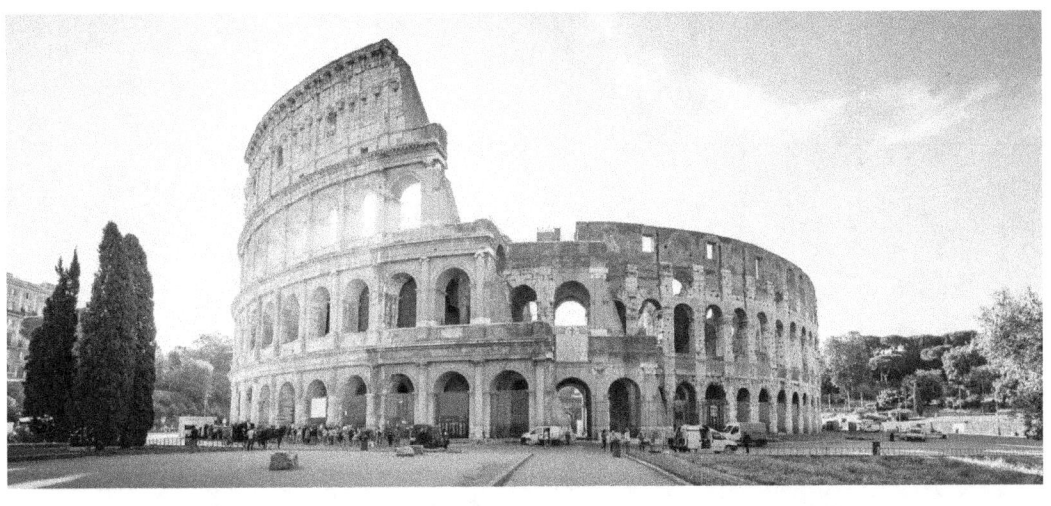

THE FORGOTTEN WONDERS OF THE WORLD

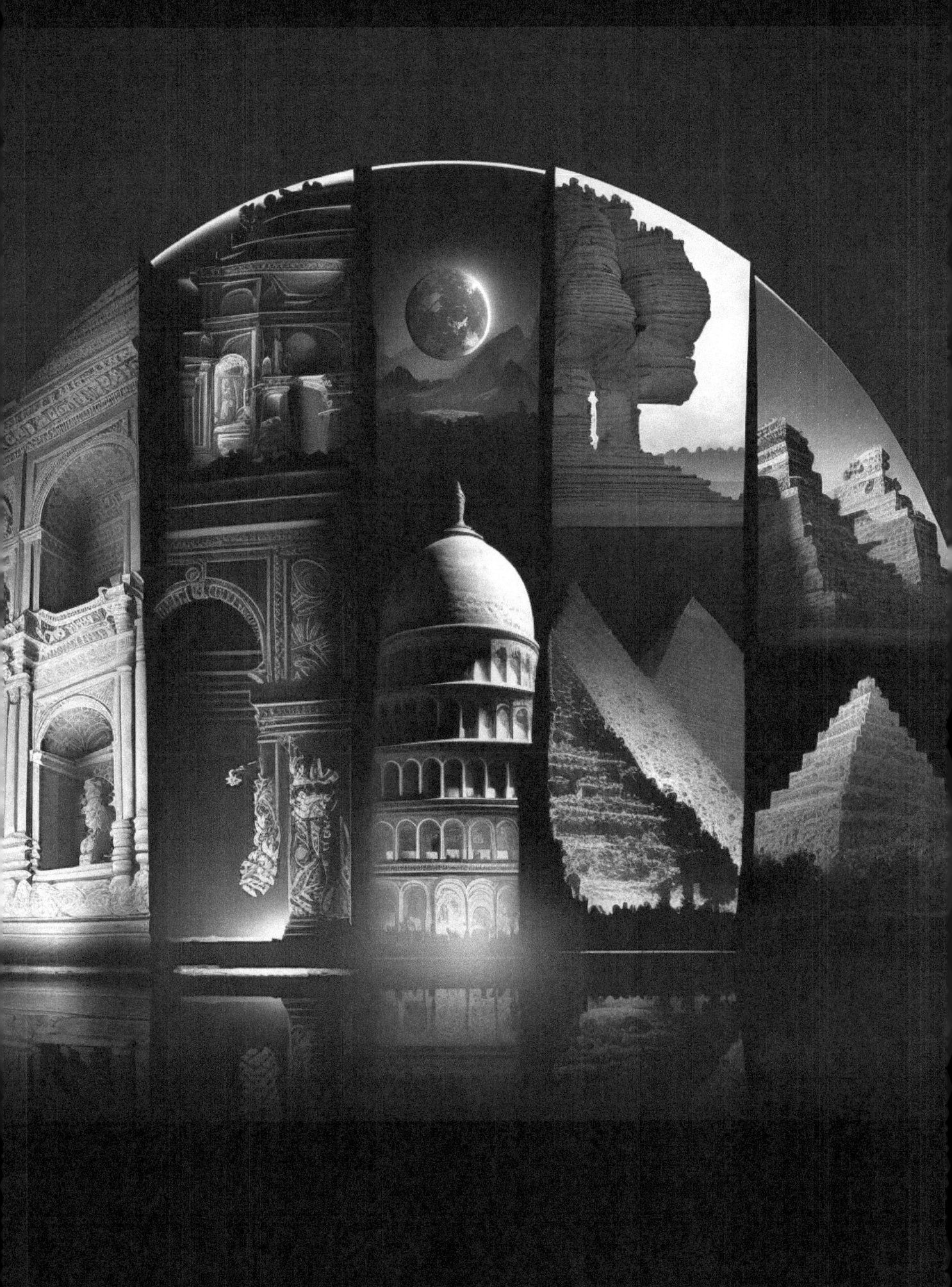

Statue of Liberty

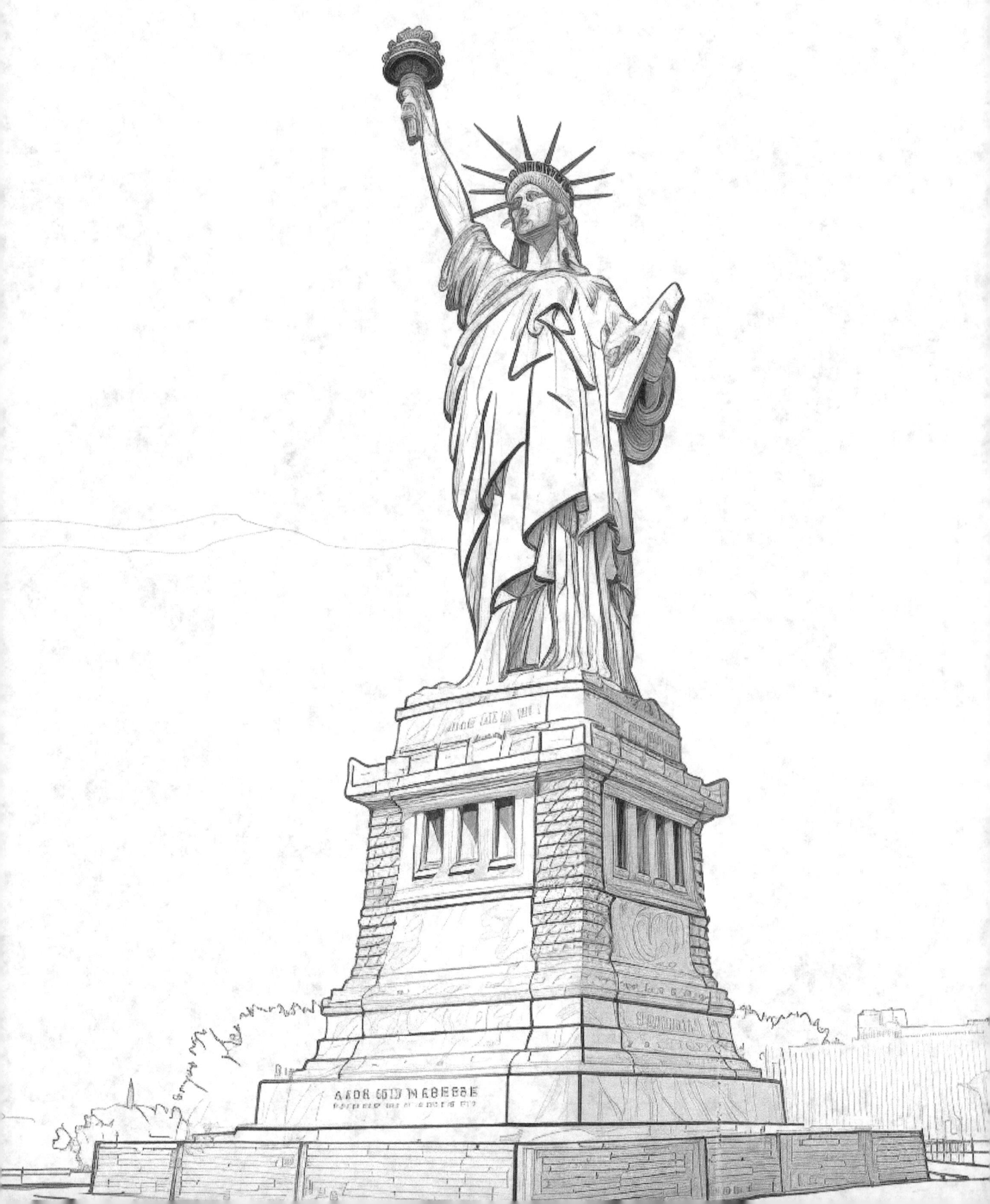

A symbol of the French-American friendship

The Statue of Liberty is an iconic American landmark located on Liberty Island in New York, United States. This statue was designed by French architect Gustave Eiffel and sculpted by Frédéric-Auguste Bartholdi. It was gifted by France to the United States as a sign of friendship and to celebrate the centennial of American independence in 1886.

The statue is made of steel and its exterior skin is made of copper. The construction method used for the statue was the lost-wax casting technique. This technique involves creating a full-size plaster model, then covering it with a layer of wax. Once the wax has hardened, a layer of plaster is applied, and the wax is melted away, leaving a cavity inside the plaster. The copper sheets are then melted and poured into the cavity to form the statue's skin.

Furthermore, the statue is also a symbol of immigration to the United States. It was erected at the entrance of the port of New York, which was the main point of entry for immigrants coming to America in the 19th century.

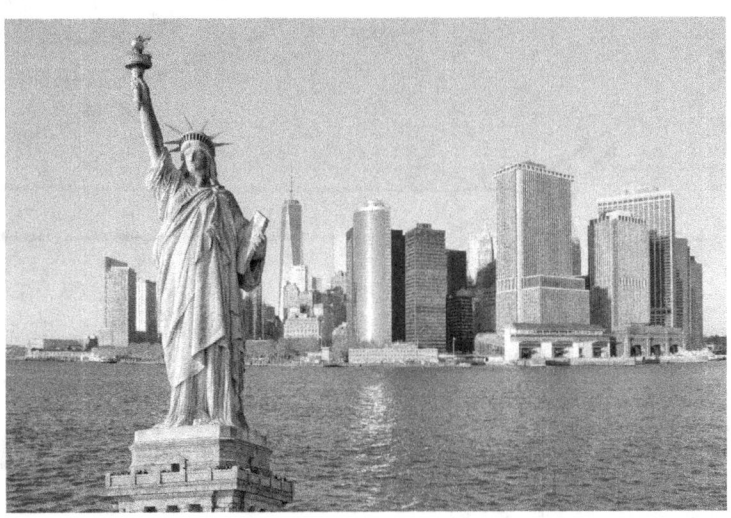

The Sydney Opera House

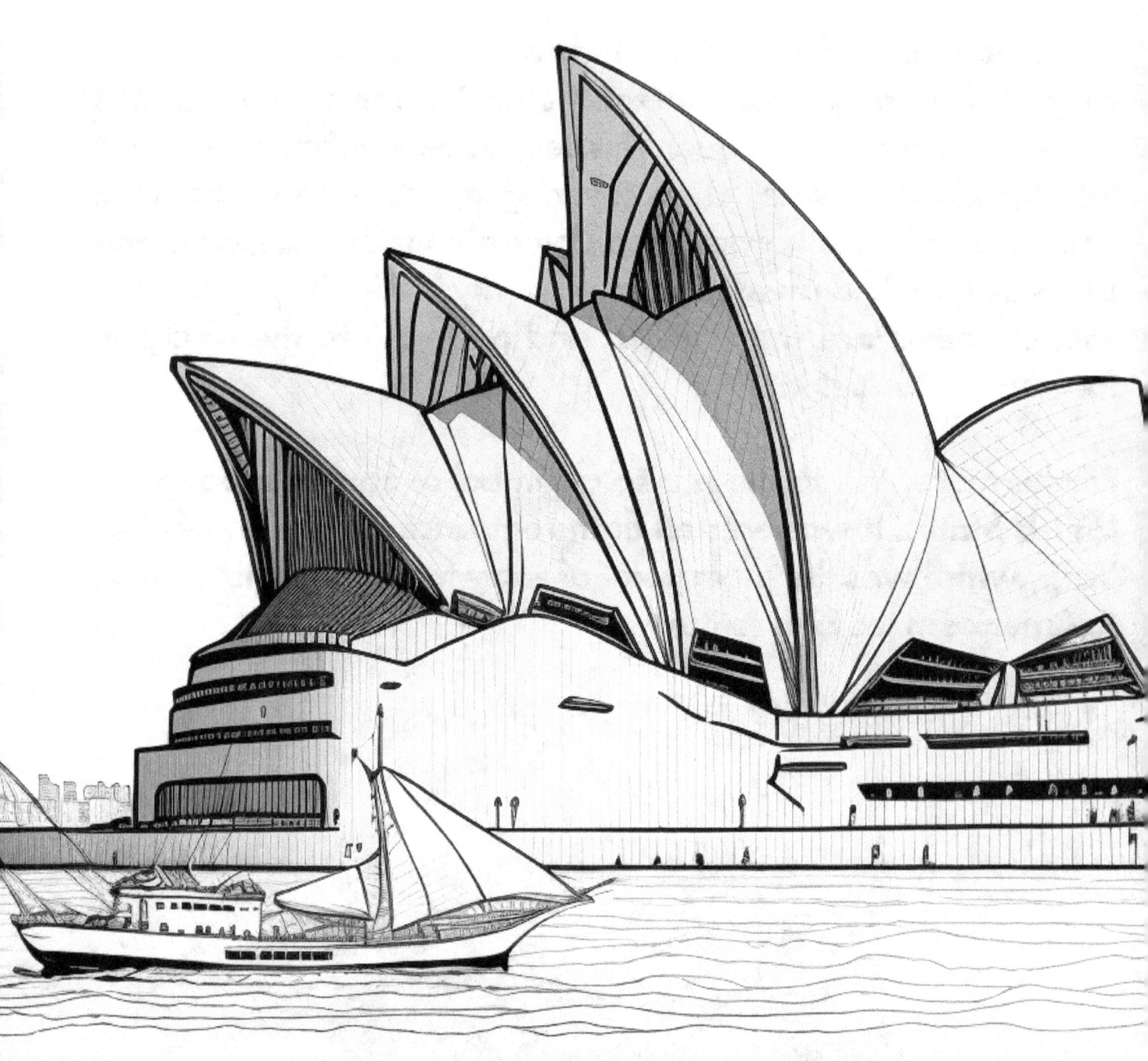

The House of Arts

The Sydney Opera House is an iconic building located on the Sydney Harbour in Australia. It has become one of the most famous tourist attractions in Australia since its opening in 1973. The Sydney Opera House was designed by Danish architect Jørn Utzon.

The roof of the building, which is composed of several sail-shaped shells, is considered one of the greatest challenges in construction. The shells are made up of over 2,500 precast concrete panels and were assembled using cranes and cables to create the distinctive shape of the opera house.

The Sydney Opera House is also known for its exceptional acoustics, which is due to a meticulous design of the concert hall. The walls of the hall are covered with specially designed wooden panels to enhance sound quality, and the shape of the building creates a natural reverberation that enhances the musical experience.

It has been listed as a UNESCO World Heritage site since 2007.

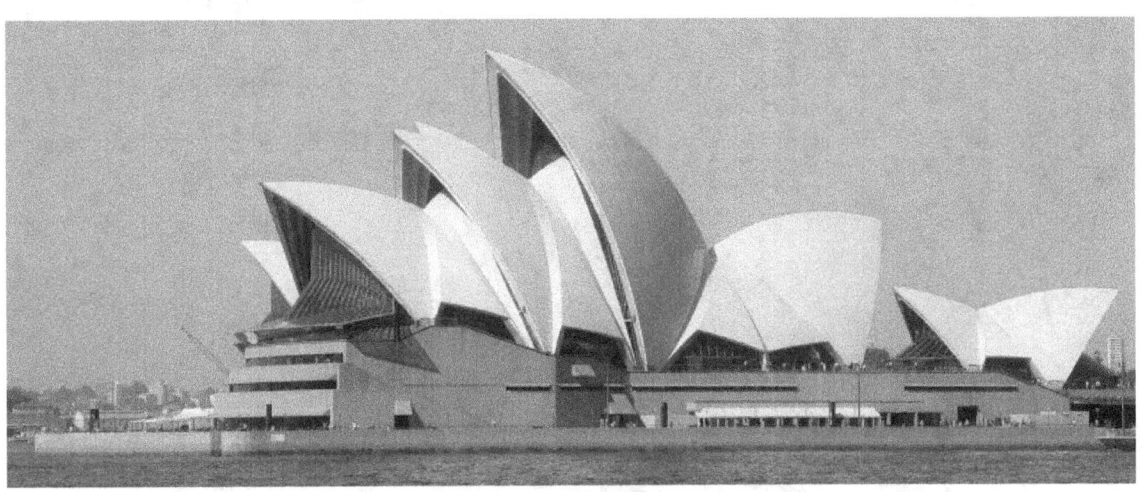

The Temples of Angkor

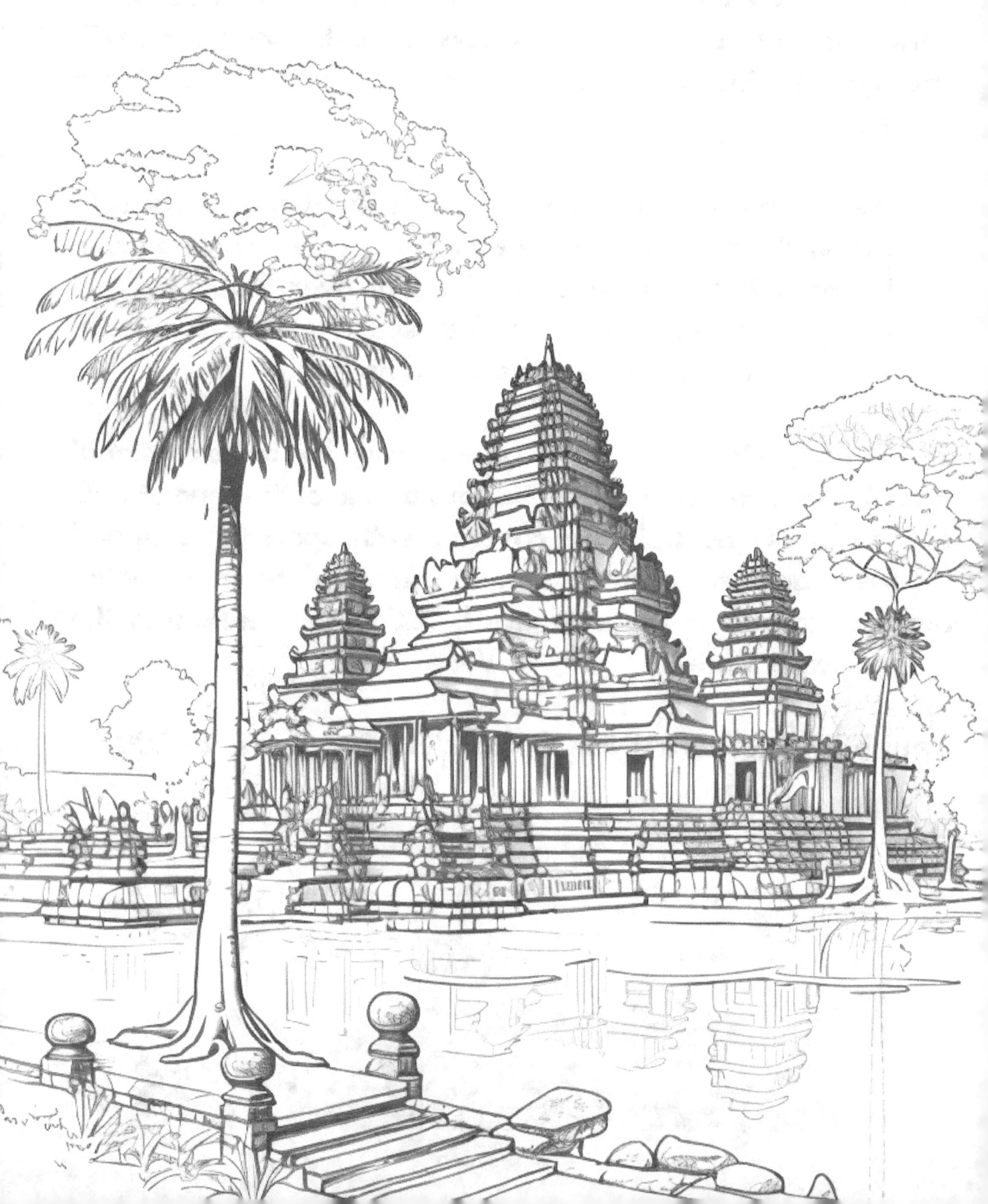

Hidden wonders of Cambodia

The Angkor temples are a collection of monumental structures located in the province of Siem Reap, Cambodia. They were built between the 9th and 15th centuries and represent one of the largest religious complexes in the world.

The most famous among them is the temple of Angkor Wat, built in the 12th century to honor the god Vishnu. It is considered one of the most beautiful examples of Khmer architecture, with its elegant central tower and water basins below.

Over the centuries, the Angkor temples were abandoned and forgotten, overtaken by the jungle. It was only in the 19th century that the temples were rediscovered and restoration efforts began. Today, the Angkor temples attract millions of visitors every year and have been classified as a UNESCO World Heritage site since 1992.

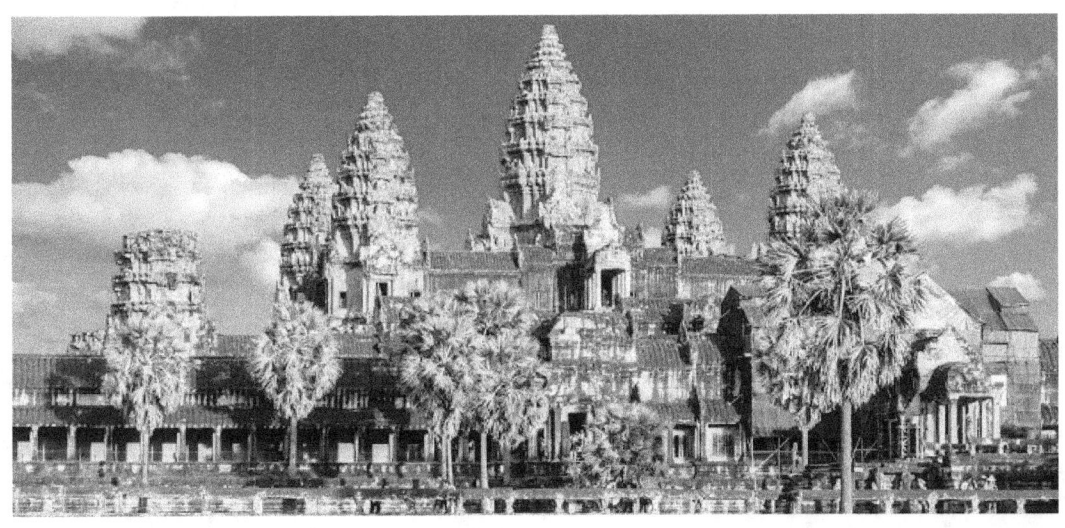

The Alhambra

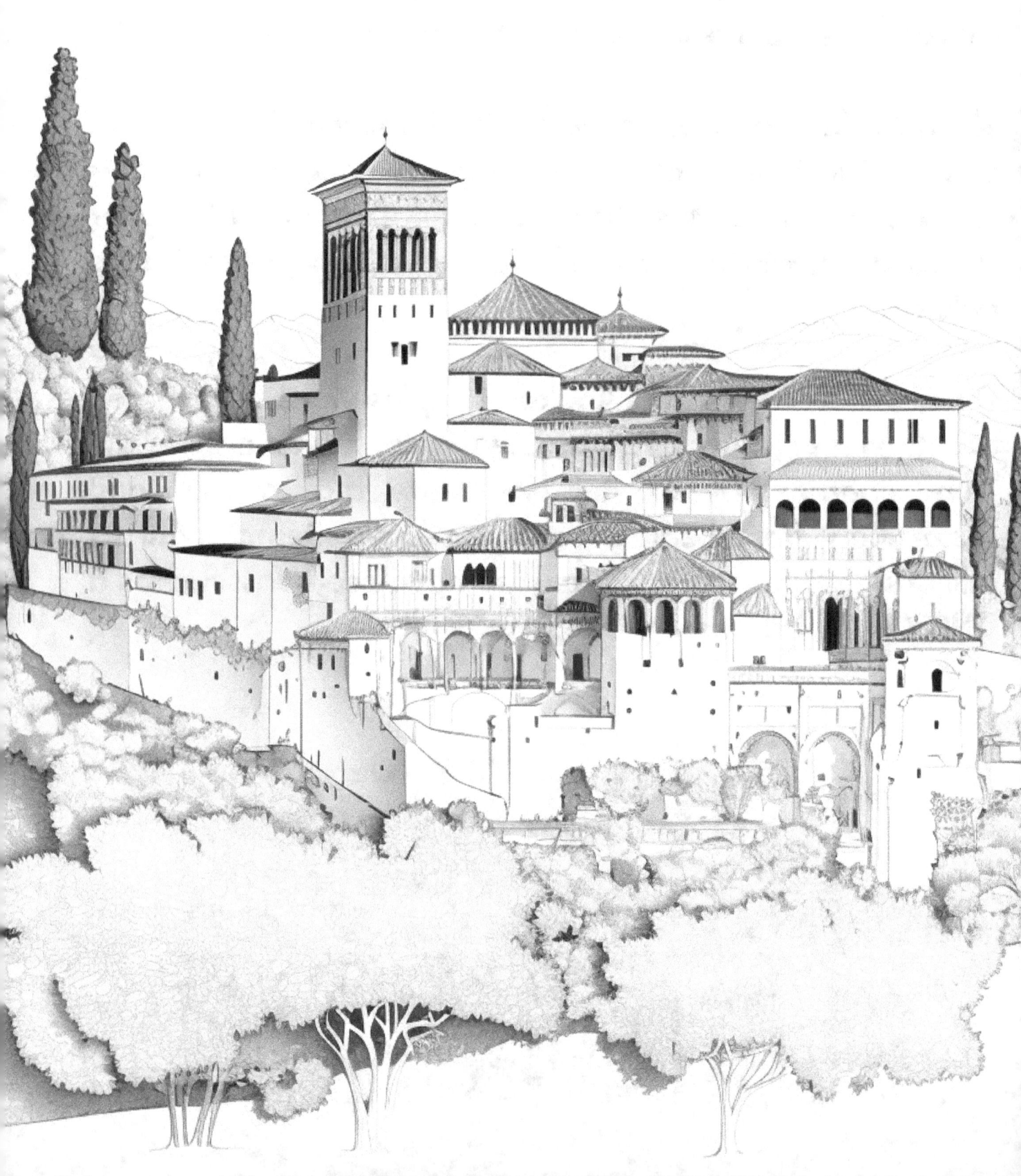

The history of the encounter between the East and the West

The Alhambra is a palace-fortress located in Granada, in the south of Spain. It was built in the 13th century by the Moorish rulers of the Nasrid dynasty and was considered one of the greatest achievements of Islamic architecture.

The Alhambra was built on a hill, which allowed for a breathtaking view of the city of Granada. It was constructed using local materials such as stone, brick, and plaster. The walls are adorned with complex geometric and floral motifs, and the rooms are decorated with ceramic mosaics.

One of the unique features of the Alhambra is the presence of water, which was integrated into the design of the complex to create a refreshing ambiance during hot summer days. Fountains and basins are fed by water channels that were built underground to bring water from the surrounding mountains.

It has also been listed as a UNESCO World Heritage Site since 1984.

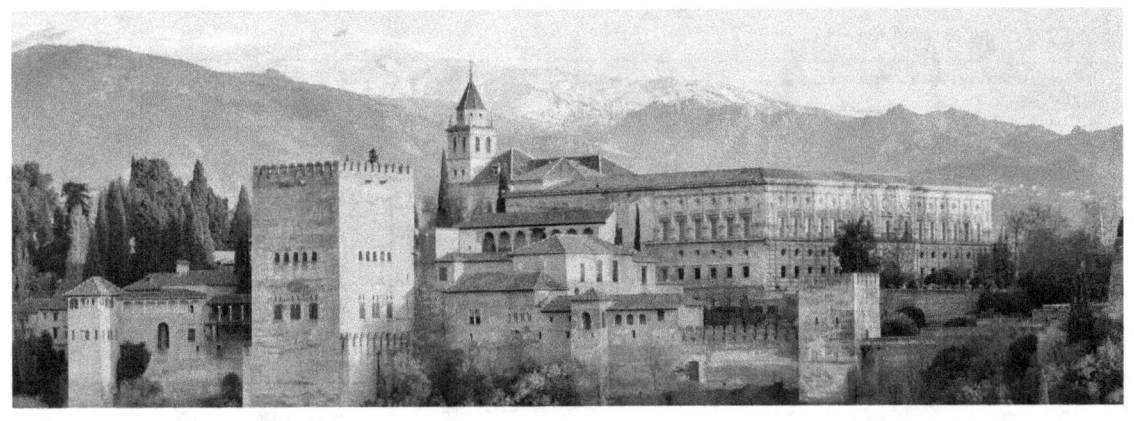

The Basilica/Mosque of Saint Sophia

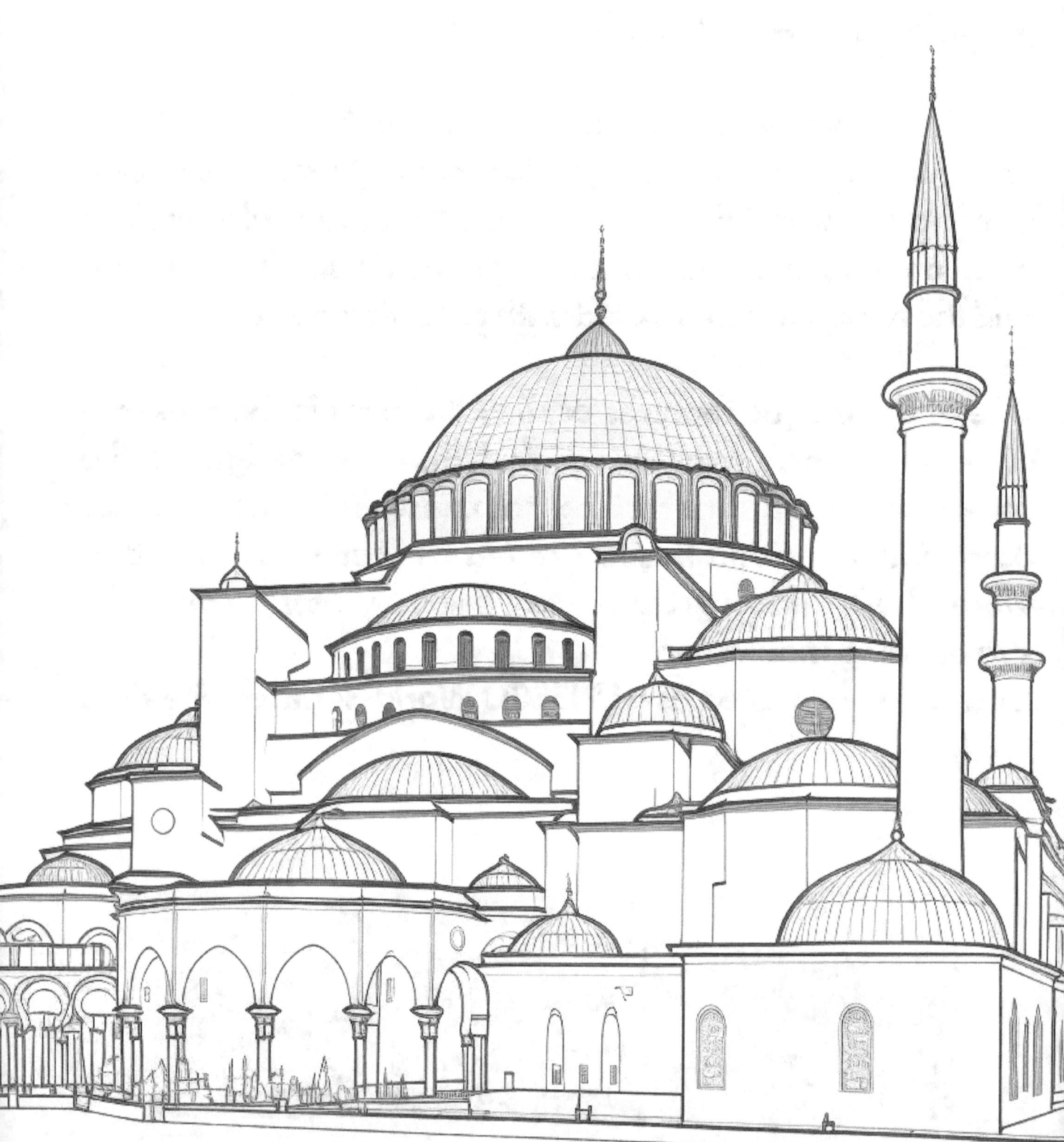

The symbol of the greatness of the Byzantine Empire

The Basilica of Saint Sophia, also known as the Mosque of Saint Sophia, is an iconic building located in Istanbul, Turkey. It was built in the 6th century under the Byzantine Empire and was used as a church for over 900 years, before being converted into a mosque by the Ottomans in the 15th century, and then into a museum in 1935.

The Basilica of Saint Sophia is an exceptional example of Byzantine architecture. The building is characterized by its large central dome, which measures nearly 32 meters in diameter, as well as its walls and arches adorned with mosaics and religious frescoes. The interior walls are covered in marble and semi-precious stones, creating an atmosphere of luxury and splendor.

In 2020, the Basilica of Saint Sophia was reconverted into a mosque by Turkish authorities, which sparked controversial reactions around the world. However, regardless of its religious affiliations, the Basilica/Mosque of Saint Sophia will remain a unique architectural and historical gem.

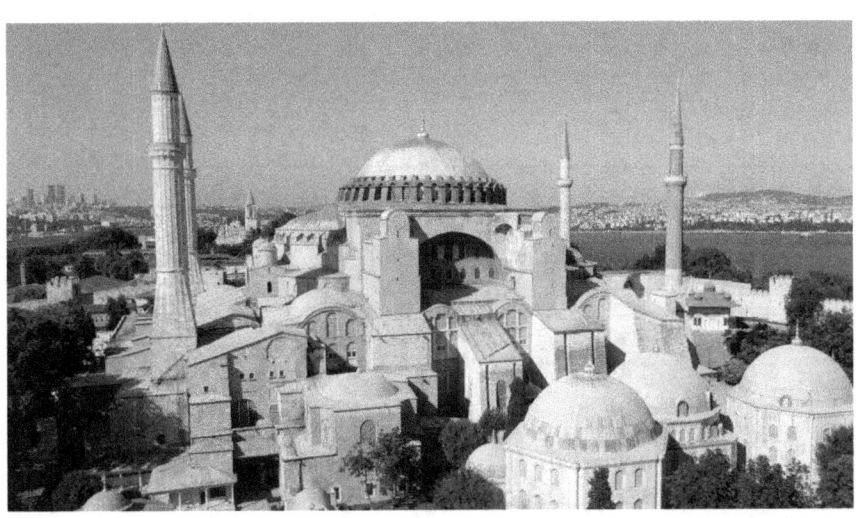

The Kremlin and Red Square

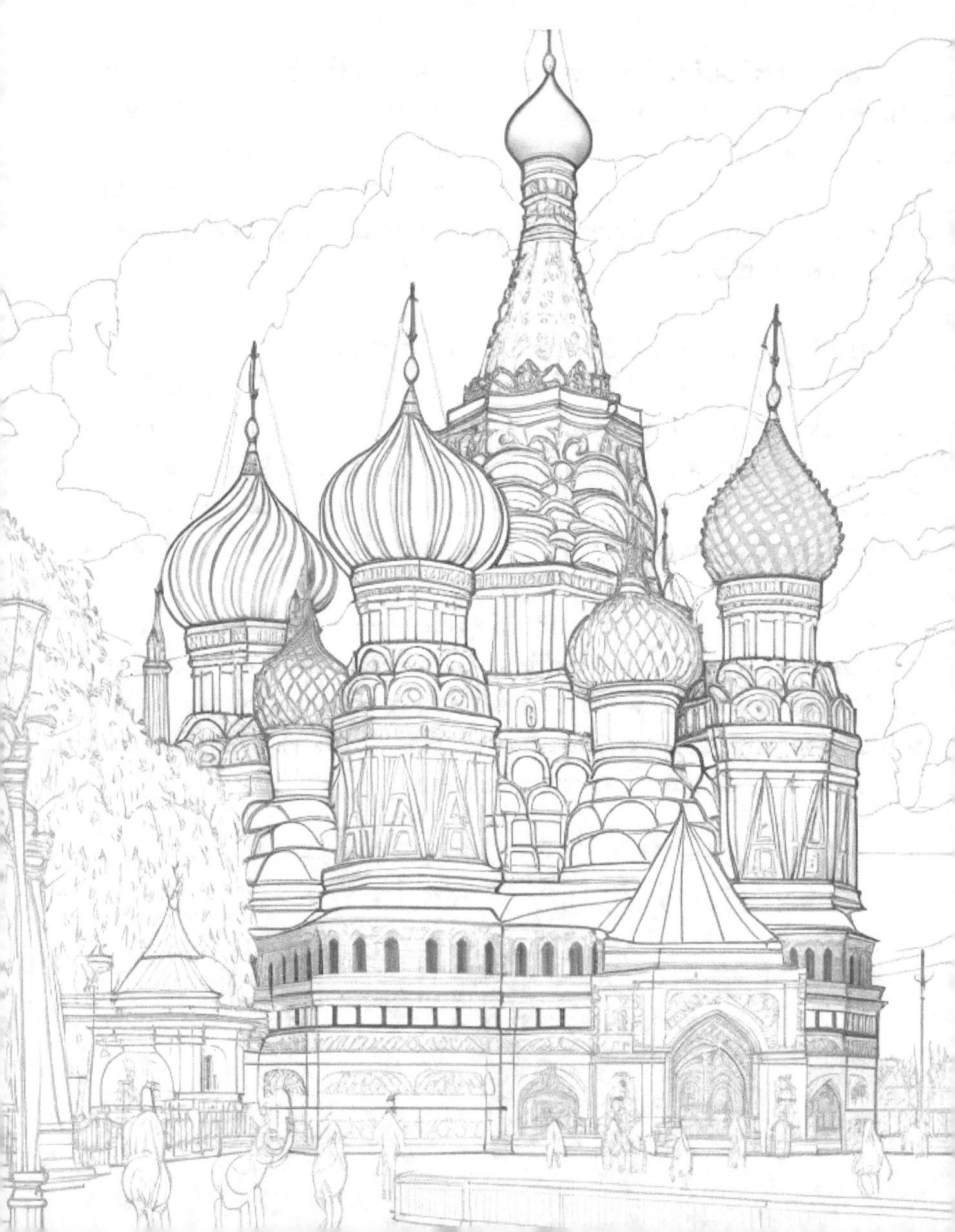

The political heart of Russia

The Kremlin and Red Square are two of the most iconic sites in Moscow, Russia. The Kremlin is a fortified complex located on the north bank of the Moskva River. It was founded in the 14th century and became the political and governmental center of Russia. The Office of the President of the Russian Federation is located in the Kremlin.

Red Square is a large paved plaza located in front of the Kremlin. It is famous for its history as a site of national celebration and military parades. It has also been the site of important historical events, such as public executions and political speeches. Red Square is lined with historic buildings, including Saint Basil's Cathedral and the Museum of Russian History.

Together, the Kremlin and Red Square represent the rich history and culture of Russia. They are symbols of Russia's power, grandeur, and wealth, as well as its glorious past.

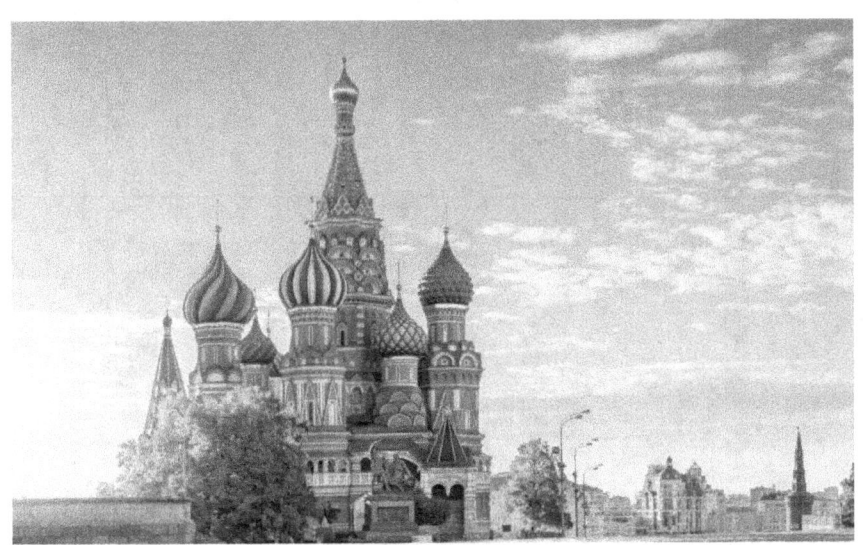

The Neuschwanstein Castle

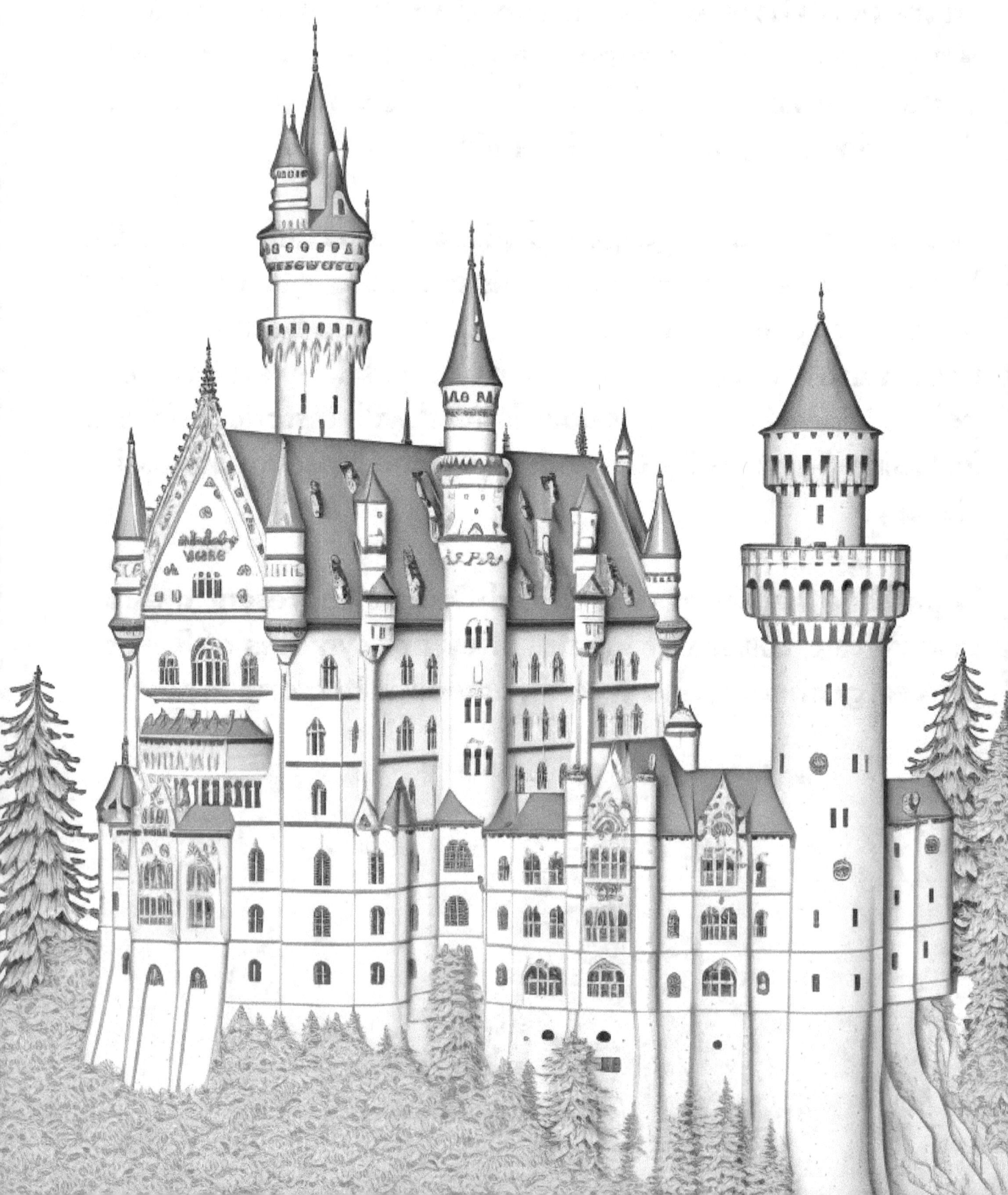

A fairy tale come true

Neuschwanstein Castle is a magnificent structure located in southern Germany near the town of Füssen. This castle was built in the 19th century by King Louis II of Bavaria in a romantic style inspired by medieval castles. It is considered one of the most beautiful castles in the world.

Neuschwanstein Castle was built between 1869 and 1886 on a hill overlooking the Ammer Valley, in the Bavarian Alps. It was designed by architect Christian Jank, but it was King Louis II himself who supervised the construction and designed most of the details.

Neuschwanstein Castle is famous for its unique architecture, beautiful interior and exterior, and rich history. It was used as a model for the famous Sleeping Beauty Castle in Disney theme parks and is one of the most popular tourist attractions in Germany. Neuschwanstein Castle remains a symbol of German history and culture.

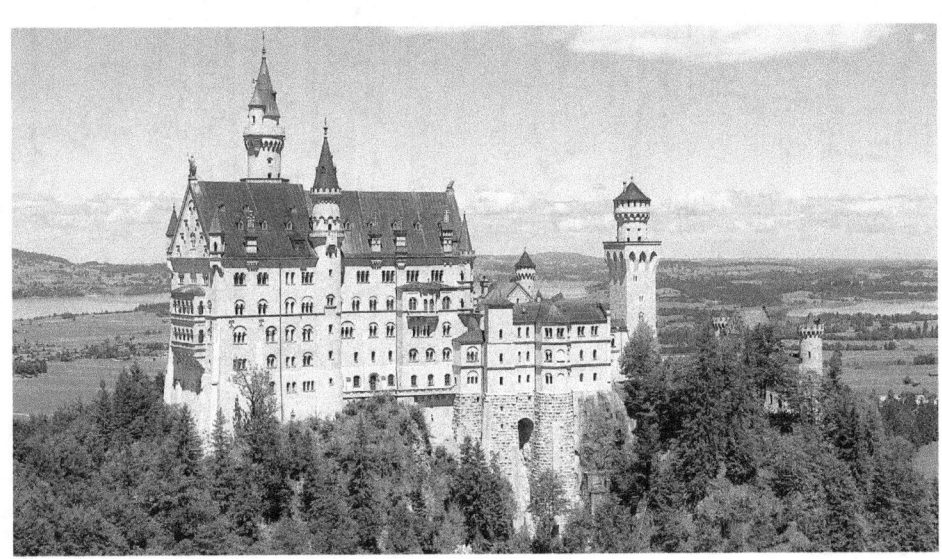

Stonehenge

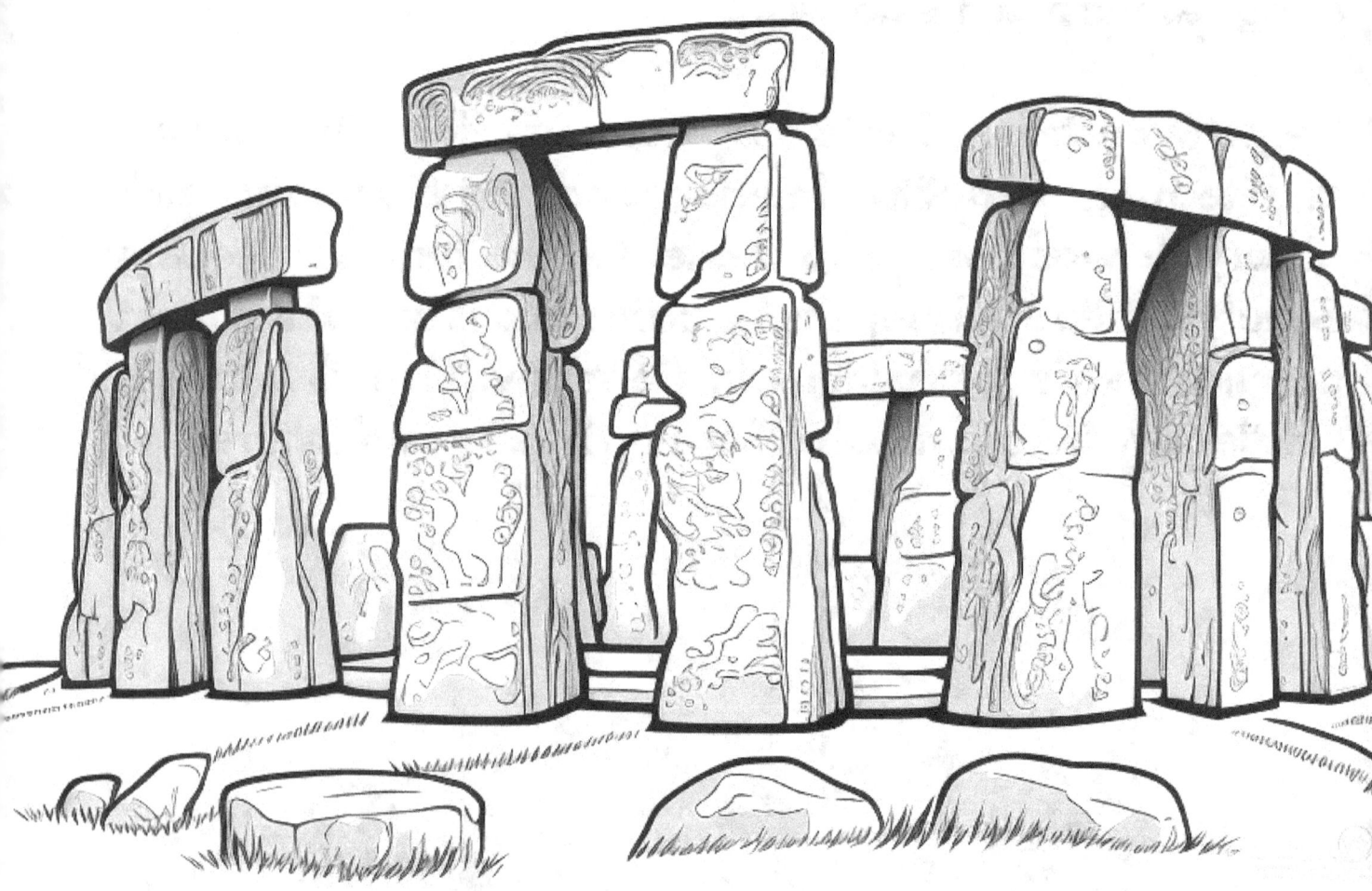

A millennial mystery that continues to fascinate

Stonehenge is a megalithic monument located in the Salisbury Plain, England. It consists of a series of upright stones arranged in concentric circles, as well as ditches and earthen banks. The monument was constructed in several phases between about 3000 and 1500 BC, during the Neolithic and Bronze Ages.

The site of Stonehenge has become one of the most famous and mysterious in the world, sparking much speculation about its meaning and purpose. It is regarded as a sacred and religious site, as well as an astronomical observatory. The stones of Stonehenge were transported over long distances, and their construction and alignment required impressive skills from their builders.

The Stonehenge monument has been on the UNESCO World Heritage list since 1986 and remains one of England's most popular tourist attractions. It continues to inspire artists, writers, and researchers from around the world, representing an extraordinary example of human ingenuity and ancient human history.

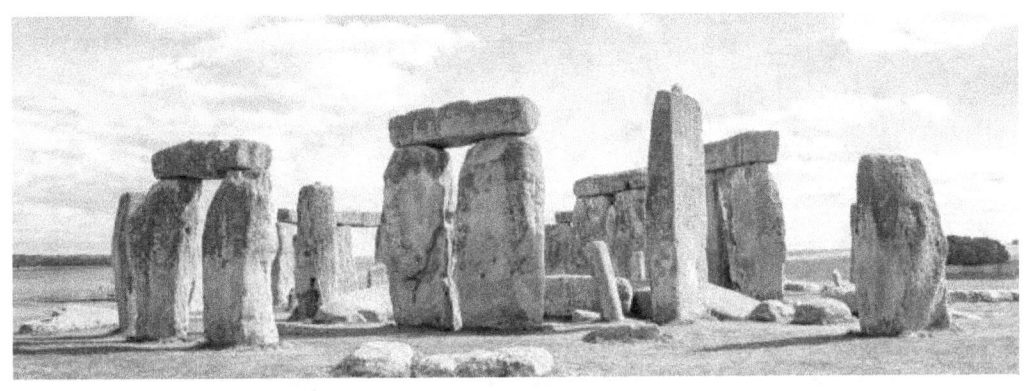

Timbuktu

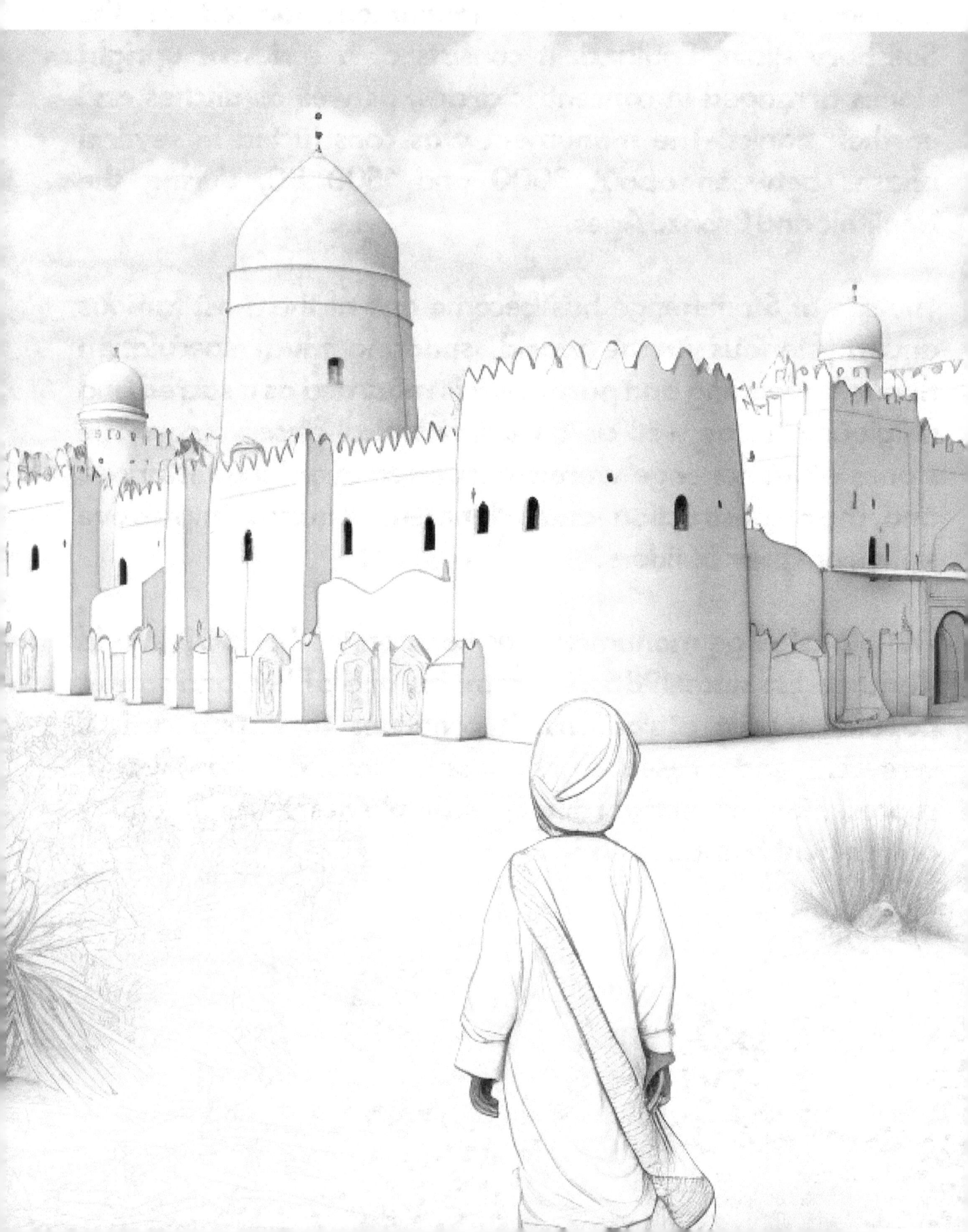

An oasis of knowledge

Timbuktu is a city located in northern Mali, at the heart of the Sahara desert. It is known to be an important cultural and commercial center of West Africa, as well as for its rich historical and cultural heritage.

The city of Timbuktu was founded in the 5th century by the Tuaregs, and reached its peak between the 11th and 16th centuries as a crossroads of trans-Saharan trade and the spread of Islamic culture in West Africa. The city was a center of learning and knowledge, with many centers of Islamic scholarship, libraries, and Quranic schools.

The architectural heritage of Timbuktu is particularly remarkable, with mosques, mausoleums, and earthen houses decorated with complex relief patterns. The city is also famous for its manuscripts, which date back several centuries and cover a variety of subjects, ranging from poetry and theology to medicine and music.

Timbuktu was inscribed on the UNESCO World Heritage List in 1988.

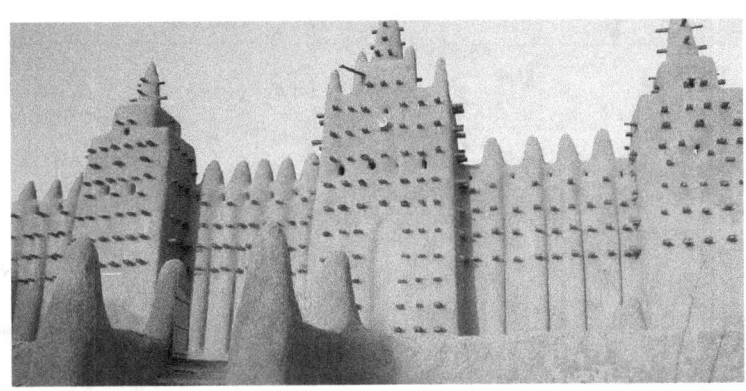

Eiffel Tower

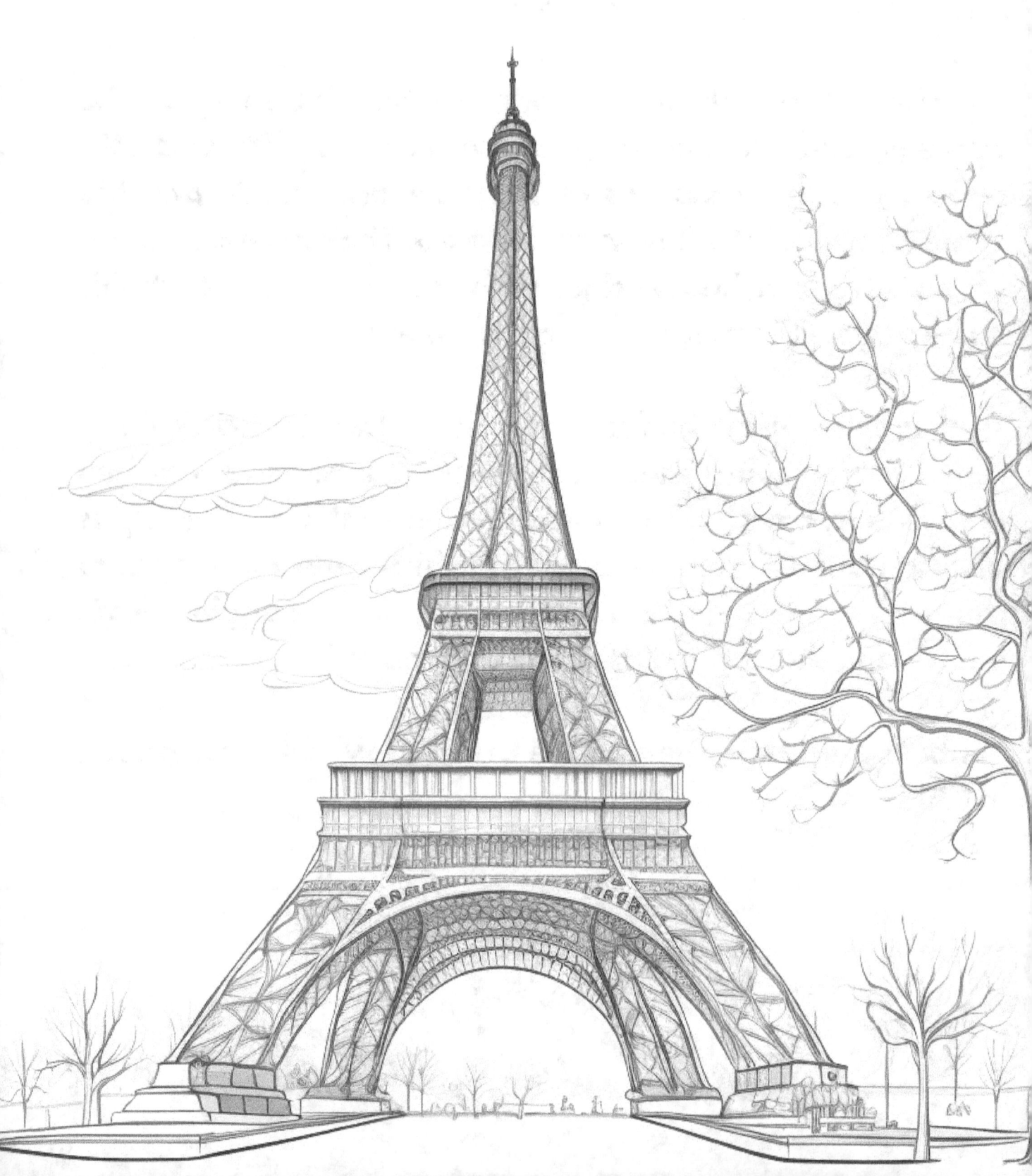

The Iron Lady

The Eiffel Tower is one of the most famous and iconic landmarks of France, located in the heart of the city of Paris. It was built in 1889 for the Universal Exposition of Paris, which marked the centenary of the French Revolution. It was designed by the French engineer Gustave Eiffel, who used wrought iron to create a tower-shaped structure that stands 324 meters tall.

The Eiffel Tower was originally intended to be a temporary construction, but it quickly won the hearts of Parisians and visitors from around the world. It is now one of the most iconic symbols of France and attracts millions of visitors every year.

The Eiffel Tower has also been used for scientific experiments, public events, and military activities. During World War II, it was used to transmit messages to the enemy and was spared from destruction thanks to its strategic value.

Today, the Eiffel Tower remains one of the most visited landmarks in the world.

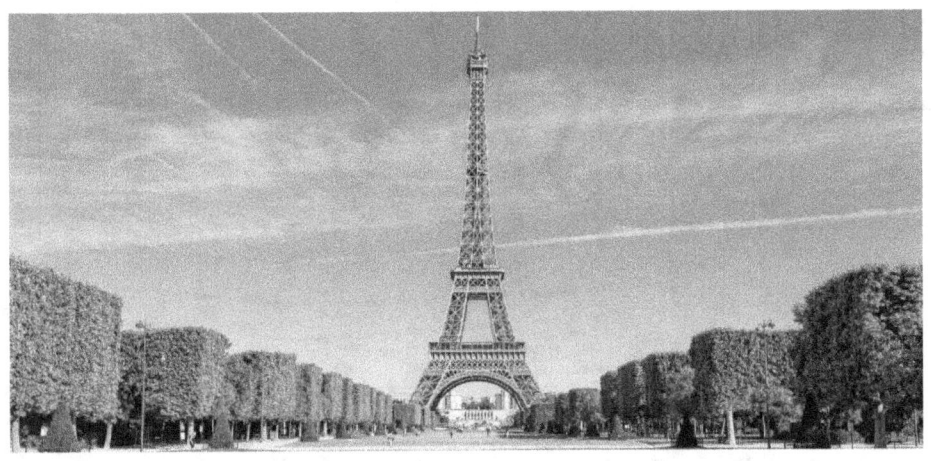

Parthenon

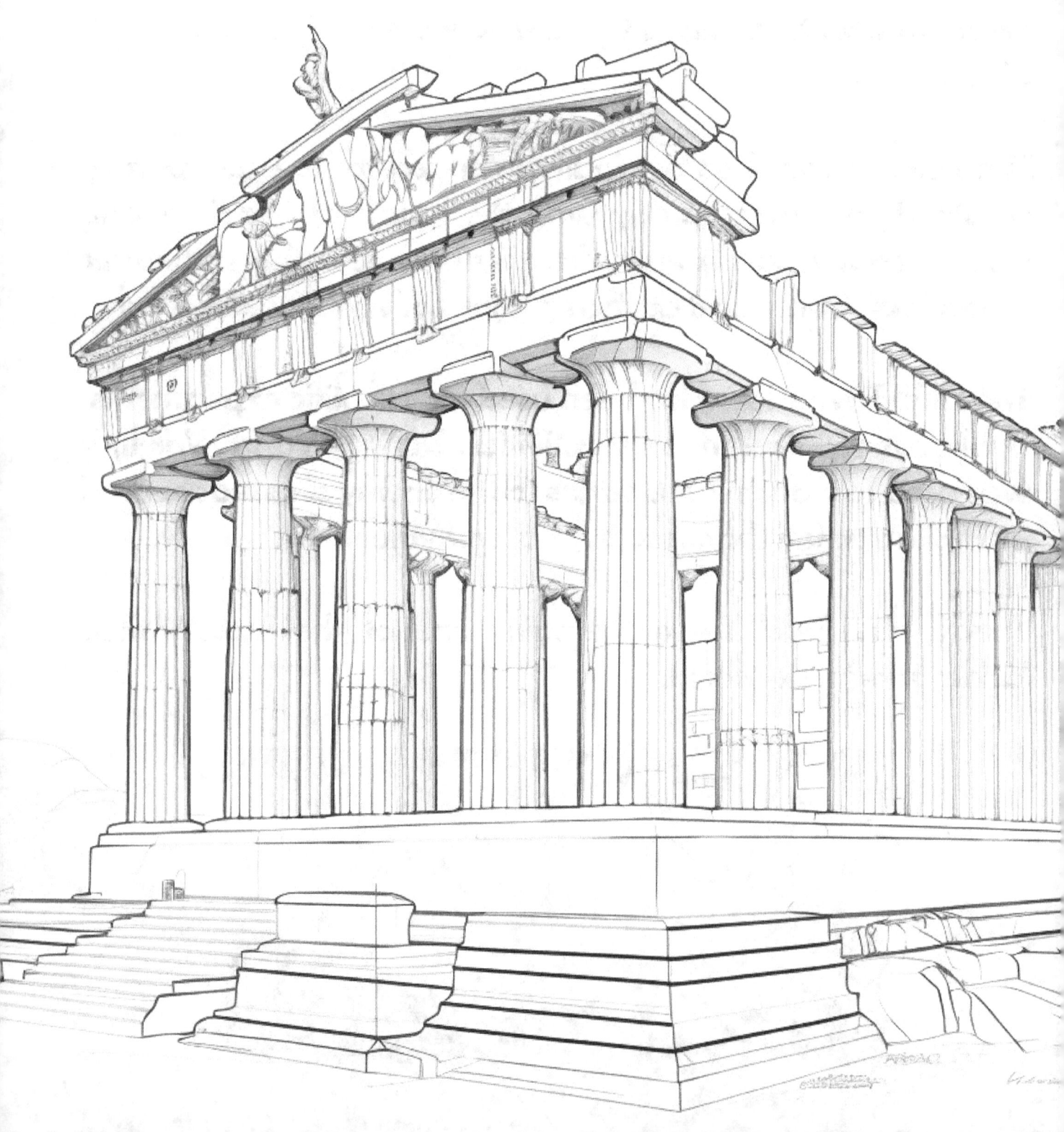

A Hellenic icon

The Parthenon is an ancient Greek temple located on the Acropolis of Athens. It was built between 447 and 432 BC during the reign of Pericles, one of the greatest leaders of the city. The temple was dedicated to the Greek goddess Athena, protector of the city of Athens.

The Parthenon is considered a masterpiece of classical Greek architecture. Its construction was supervised by the architect Ictinus and the sculptor Phidias, who used Pentelic marble to create an impressive structure. The temple is famous for its Doric columns, which have inspired many other constructions around the world.

In 1687, an accidental gunpowder explosion caused significant damage to the temple. The sculptures of the pediment were damaged and the columns were overturned. The Parthenon was inscribed on the UNESCO World Heritage list in 1987.

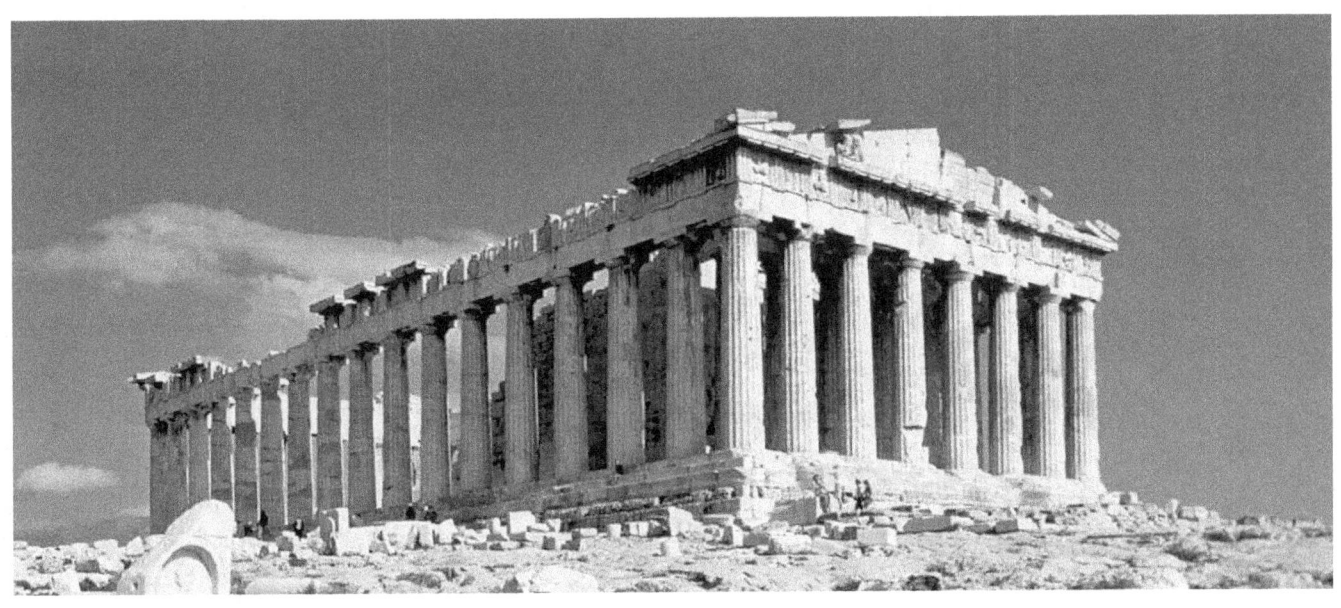

It's your turn : What would your wonder of the world look like ?